SEMINAR STUDIES IN HISTORY

The Dissolution of the Austro-Hungarian Empire, 1867–1918

SEMINAR STUDIES IN HISTORY

General Editor: Roger Lockyer

The Dissolution of the Austro-Hungarian Empire, 1867–1918

John W. Mason

Lecturer in History
Bournville College of Further Education

LONGMAN
London and New York

LONGMAN GROUP UK LIMITED
Longman House, Burnt Mill, Harlow, Essex CM20 2JE, UK and
Associated Companies throughout the world.
Published in the United States of America by Longman Inc., New York

First published 1985
Fourth impression 1992
ISBN 0 582 35393 9

Set in 10/11pt Linotron Baskerville

Produced by Longman Singapore Publishers Pte Ltd
Printed in Singapore

For Josephine, Sam and Eliza

The Publisher's policy is to use paper manufactured from
sustainable forests.

British Library Cataloguing in Publication Data

Mason, John W.
  The dissolution of the Austro-Hungarian
  Empire, 1867–1918. — (Seminar studies in history)
  1. Austria — History — 1867–1918
  2. Hungary — History — 1867–1918
  I. Title
  943.6′04   DB85

  ISBN 0–582–35393–9

Library of Congress in Publication Data

Mason, John W.
  The dissolution of the Austro-Hungarian Empire, 1867–1918.

  (Seminar studies in history)
  Bibliography: p.
  Includes index.
    1. Austria — History — 1867–1918.   I. Title.   II. Series.
  DB86.M36 1985   943.6′04   84–17137 ISBN 0–582–35393–9

Contents

Seminar Studies in History

Founding Editor: Patrick Richardson

Introduction

The Seminar Studies series was conceived by Patrick Richardson, whose experience of teaching history persuaded him of the need for something more substantial than a textbook chapter but less formidable than the specialised full-length academic work. He was also convinced that such studies, although limited in length, should provide an up-to-date and authoritative introduction to the topic under discussion as well as a selection of relevant documents and a comprehensive bibliography.

Patrick Richardson died in 1979, but by that time the Seminar Studies series was firmly established, and it continues to fulfil the rôle he intended for it. This book, like others in the series, is therefore a living tribute to a gifted and original teacher.

Note on the System of References:
A bold number in round brackets (**5**) in the text refers the reader to the corresponding entry in the Bibliography section at the end of the book. A bold number in square brackets, preceded by 'doc' [**doc. 6 8**] refers the reader to the corresponding item in the section of Documents, which follows the main text.

ROGER LOCKYER
General Editor

Acknowledgements

We are grateful for permission to reproduce the following material: table on page 97 from O. Jaszi, *The Dissolution of the Habsburg Monarchy*, University of Chicago Press, 1929; table on page 85 and map on page x from Robert A. Kann, *A History of the Habsburg Empire 1526–1918*, University of California Press, 1974; table on page 86 from P. Vysny, *Neo-Slavism and the Czechs, 1898–1914*, Cambridge University Press, 1977; tables on pages 87 and 88 from R.L. Rudolph, *Banking and Industrialization in Austria-Hungary, The role of the banks in the industrialization of the Czech Crownlands, 1873–1914*, Cambridge University Press, 1976; tables on pages 87 and 88 from Adam Wandruszka and Peter Urbanitsch, *Die Habsburgermonarchie, 1848–1918*, Österreichische Akademie der Wissenschaften.

Cover: from *Interessanten Blatt*, the murder attempt of Franz Ferdinand in Sarajevo on 28 June 1914. Drawing by Felix Schwormstädt. Bild-Archiv der Österreichischen Nationalbibliothek, Wien.

Foreword

The Austro-Hungarian Empire is one of the great lost causes of modern European history. Yet lost causes have perhaps as much to tell us as successes in history. The central problem of the Habsburg Monarchy in its last fifty years (1867–1918) was how a multi-national empire, knit together by dynastic ties, could adjust and survive in an age of nationalism and democracy. Four specific internal problems can be identified: (1) the failure to solve the Czech-German conflict in the 1880s and 1890s; (2) the failure to develop a genuine parliamentary government in the late 1890s; (3) the failure to solve the Austrian-Hungarian conflict in the early 1900s; (4) the failure to solve the South Slav conflict in the decade before World War One.

Domestic failure led to foreign-policy disaster. On 28 June 1914 the heir-apparent to the Habsburg throne, Franz Ferdinand, was shot in Sarajevo by a Bosnian nationalist. This event sparked off World War One and the war caused the Monarchy to collapse in 1918. The Habsburg Monarchy was certainly not in a healthy state before 1914. But it would be a great mistake to see it as foredoomed to fall because of our knowledge of what happened to it in the last year of the war.

The same empire which struggled with these political problems formed the seed-bed of many of the most important ideas and cultural achievements of the twentieth century. In Vienna Zionism, as well as its opposite, racial anti-semitism, was born. The young Adolf Hitler acquired his earliest political education on the streets of the polyglot capital in the early years of the twentieth century. Vienna, more than any other city in Europe, epitomised the break-down of liberalism at the time and paved the way for the mass movements in politics and the beginnings of the 'modern' movement in music, art, literature, psychology and philosophy.

I wish to thank both Roger Lockyer for his helpful editorial guidance and the British Academy for a Humanities grant, which enabled me to undertake research in Vienna in the summer of 1983.

John W. Mason

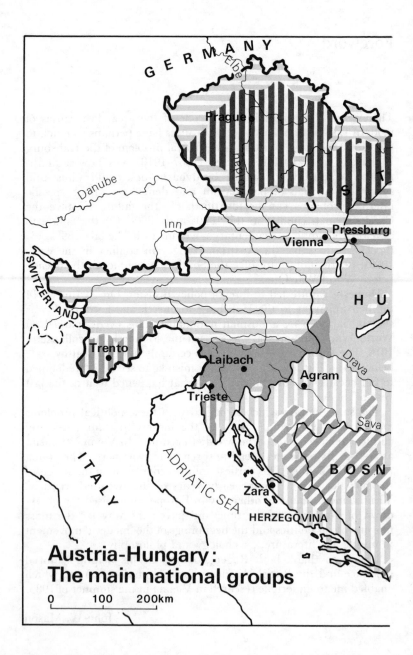

Austria-Hungary:
The main national groups

0   100   200km

x

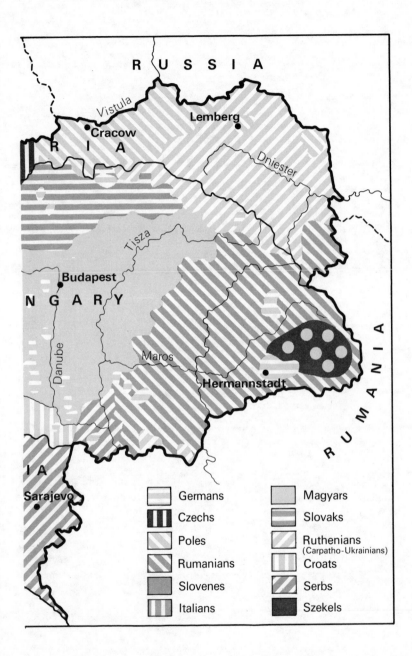

Germans
Czechs
Poles
Rumanians
Slovenes
Italians
Magyars
Slovaks
Ruthenians
(Carpatho-Ukrainians)
Croats
Serbs
Szekels

Part One: The Background

1 The Habsburg Monarchy in European History

The Habsburg Monarchy existed for over 600 years as a unique political unit in European history. Founded in 1278 as a dynastic creation, it was dissolved in 1918 as a dynastic creation, never having become linked to a single nation. In 1867, when the Monarchy divided into two separate states, Austria and Hungary, the so-called Dual Monarchy consisted of no less than eleven national groups: Germans, Magyars, Poles, Italians, Croats, Czechs, Slovaks, Serbs, Slovenes, Ruthenians and Rumanians. In proportion to its size the Habsburg realm displayed, in L.B. Namier's words, 'more frontier and less coherence than any other State in Europe' (**156**).

The period covered in this book – the last fifty years of the Monarchy, 1867 to 1918 – was a time of political decay and disintegration, but also one of economic growth and extraordinary cultural efflorescence. Although it was the final phase of the Monarchy, the Habsburgs themselves regarded it as just another phase in the rule of their dynasty. Their very survival into the age of nationalism and democracy in the nineteenth and twentieth centuries was seen by many, both inside and outside the Monarchy, as the surest basis of their continued existence. Why that Monarchy failed and what it achieved before the final collapse in 1918 are the subjects of this book.

From the origins of the House of Habsburg to 1848

The name Habsburg derives from *Habichtsburg*, 'the Castle of the Hawks', situated in what is today the Swiss canton of Aargau. From about the eleventh century the knights of the castle rose to a position of influence in southern Germany by forming alliances with many of the families in the area. Meanwhile, the eastern march (i.e., *Oesterreich*, or in Latin *Austria*) of Charlemagne's empire was granted to the Babenberg family in the tenth century and they held it for the next 300 years (**20**). In 1273 the imperial electors of the Holy Roman Empire elected Rudolf of Habsburg to the office of German

Emperor. From their humble origins in the Swiss mountains the Habsburgs had become a Danubian power on the edge of German-speaking territory with future ambitions directed towards Bohemia, Hungary and south-east Europe.

The Habsburgs gradually increased the power of their house (the *Hausmacht*) by adding to the territory under their rule. In the four-teenth century they acquired Carinthia, Carniola, Tyrol, Istria and Trieste. In the following century the Habsburgs were elected Holy Roman Emperors and the crown remained in their house almost continuously from 1438 until the end of the Empire in 1806. The foundations for a world empire (including the Spanish Netherlands, Bohemia and Hungary) were laid by a series of dynastic marriages. When King Louis II of Bohemia and Hungary died without issue in 1526 in the battle of Mohács against the Turks, the Habsburgs inherited his two crowns.

The acquisition of Bohemia and Hungary in 1526 (and Croatia in 1527) marked a turning point in the development of the Habsburg Monarchy (**10**). The hereditary lands which had made up the Empire before 1526 were predominantly German in character and therefore could be quite easily integrated under the crown. The new kingdoms of the east, by contrast, were mainly non-German and had long-established independent histories. From the start then, Habs-burg rule in the eastern territories had to rest on the free decisions of their own privileged representative assemblies. One significant re-sult of these gains was that the Habsburg Monarchy began to take a different historical path from the countries in western Europe. Just at the time when the nation-state was emerging as the primary unit in the West, the multi-national empire was becoming established as the norm in eastern Europe (**11**, **74**).

The enormous problems of governing a multi-national empire lay in the future. In the sixteenth and seventeenth centuries the Habs-burg rulers were preoccupied with defending central Europe against two distinct enemies: the Turks from without and the Protestants from within. Austria's struggles against these foes unified the Empire, gave it a *raison d'être* and in the view of some historians lent it a particular character which it never lost (**2**, **10**). Twice in these years – first in 1529 and again in 1683 – the Turks laid siege to Vienna, but each time they were driven back by the Habsburg armies. In the process the Habsburg Empire consolidated its posi-tion as a Great Power.

The Habsburg Monarchy emerged as a great European power in the early eighteenth century. The long struggle against the Ottoman

Empire had ended in favour of the Habsburgs; henceforth, their main function in Europe would be to act as 'the great counterpoise to France' (**3**). In the War of Spanish Succession (1702–14) Prince Eugene of Savoy, the most heroic military figure in Austrian history, joined with the Duke of Marlborough to defeat the French and won for the dynasty the Spanish Netherlands and the richest provinces of Italy.

Under Maria Theresa (1740–80) and her son, Joseph II (1780–90), the Empire became a centralised administrative system for the first time (**15**). Hungary, however, retained its constitutional independence and privileges, in spite of attempts by Joseph to crush them. At this time Austria's leading position in central Europe was contested by Hohenzollern Prussia, which under Frederick the Great took the rich German-speaking province of Silesia from Austria. Austria received some compensation for his loss by taking Galicia in the first partition of Poland in 1772. But Prussia was now a threat to the Habsburg Monarchy and there was no way in which the latter could sustain a struggle against her northern rival without the support of Hungary (**16**). The price that had to be paid was concessions to Hungary. We can see foreshadowed here the shape of relations between Austria and Hungary under the Dual Monarchy from 1867.

The French Revolution and the twenty years of war it unleashed had a profound effect on the Habsburg Monarchy. Two of the main ideas of the French Revolution – nationalism and political democracy –struck at the very roots of the multinational Habsburg Empire; it now became the ideological opponent of the new order which France, under Napoleon, was seeking to impose on all Europe. When Napoleon assumed the title of Emperor of the French in 1804, Francis II (1792–1835) responded by proclaiming himself Emperor of Austria. The Habsburgs had been elected Holy Roman Emperors for centuries, but in 1806 the Holy Roman Empire was dissolved and henceforth they became hereditary Austrian Emperors. Although the change of title did not affect the internal position of the various states, it registered the shift of the centre of the House of Austria away from Germany towards the east (**11**). In the words of V.L. Tapié, 'modern Austria had been born' (**20**).

After Napoleon's final defeat in 1813 the victors met in Vienna, which became the diplomatic capital of Europe. The Habsburgs assumed the leadership of the loose German Confederation and took over two rich territories in Italy – Lombardy and Venetia. But behind the outward strength and dedication to absolute rule the

empire was weak and unable to cope with the new forces of liberalism and nationalism. Metternich served as foreign minister from
1809, and as chancellor from 1829 to 1848, and his name became the
symbol of the age which culminated in the revolutions of 1848.
Metternich's aim was to preserve the territorial *status quo* and uphold
the old patriarchal system of government; the means he used were
an enlarged police force, censorship and political repression (**14**).

The period of constitutional experiments: 1848–67

The period 1848–67 was a crucial and formative one in the history of
the Habsburg Monarchy. Internal revolution, foreign wars and
constitutional crises left the Monarchy in a weakened position in
1867. The 1848 revolutions shook most countries in Europe to their
foundations. But they had a greater impact on Austria than else-
where because there the government had to face a nationalist challenge in addition to the democratic one. What happened in Austria
in 1848 and after was that national aspirations conflicted with
liberal claims and the latter lost. One of the tragedies of central
Europe in the mid-nineteenth century was that national unity took
precedence over liberty (**21, 156**).

In 1848 five separate, but interrelated revolutions took place
within the Habsburg Empire: the German (in Vienna), the Czech
(in Prague), the Magyar (in Budapest), the Croat (in Agram) and
the Italian (in Milan and Venice) (**14**). Metternich was forced to
resign, the court had to leave Vienna, and the Monarchy was
momentarily thrown off balance. But the Habsburg armies under
Marshall Radetsky and Prince Windischgrätz soon crushed the
rebel forces in Prague, Vienna, Budapest and Italy. Hungary, which
had proclaimed an independent republic in 1849, was forced to
capitulate when the Russian army came to the aid of Austria and
defeated the Hungarian forces at Világos in the same year. Hungary's defeat at the hands of Russia was never forgotten by the
Magyars and was crucial in shaping their future relationship with
Austria.

By 1850 the Habsburg Empire had regained her position of leadership in Italy and Germany. In December 1848 the feeble Emperor
Ferdinand (1835–48) abdicated in favour of his 18-year-old nephew,
Franz Joseph, who was to rule for the next 68 years. Franz Joseph
fell under the sway of Prince Schwarzenberg, who led the return to
absolutist, centralised rule until his death in 1852. His work was
carried on by Alexander Bach in the 1850s (**15**).

Franz Joseph owed the survival of his dynasty to the army in 1848–49; by the same logic the defeats of the army in separate wars against France in 1859 and Prussia in 1866 left the Monarchy in a weakened position in 1867 (**6**). Austria maintained a neutral position during the Crimean War (1853–56), fought between Russia and the two western powers, Britain and France. She thereby isolated herself diplomatically and was unable to resist changes in Italy and Germany in 1859 and 1866, when they were backed by the French and Prussian armies respectively (**130**).

In 1859, France, in support of Piedmont, defeated Austria in the battles of Magenta and Solferino and forced Austria to cede Lombardy. One result of these defeats was a financial and constitutional crisis within Austria which forced her to introduce a constitutional government in 1860–61. But the constitution of 1861, which emphasised the unitary character of the Habsburg Empire, satisfied neither the nationalists nor the liberals. More important, the Magyars opposed the constitution from the beginning and were eventually able to wring concessions from Franz Joseph when Austria once again found herself in a foreign-policy crisis with Germany in 1865 (**14**). Austria had hoped to ally with Prussia in 1860 in a crusade against France to recover Lombardy. But Prussia – which, since 1862, had been under its new prime minister, Bismarck – had other plans. He hoped to win over the states in the German Confederation from Austrian control. Austria now found herself isolated: Italy allied with Prussia, while France and Russia remained neutral (**20**).

Austria suffered a devastating defeat at the hands of Prussia in the battle of Sadowa in 1866. The Treaty of Prague (1866) sealed the exclusion of the Habsburg Monarchy from Germany, thus ending 600 years of history. Further, it marked the triumph of German (and Magyar) nationalism in central Europe and ended all attempts to find a federal solution to the problem of governing an empire of many nationalities. The final constitutional transformation of the Habsburg Monarchy into the Austro-Hungarian Empire in 1867 was determined by the Prussian needle gun on the battlefield of Sadowa (**21**).

2 1867 – The Austro-Hungarian Compromise

The Compromise (*Ausgleich*) of 1867 recognised the sovereign equality of the two states - Austria and Hungary – and brought them together under a common ruler, Franz Joseph, as emperor in Austria and king in Hungary. This ended the long period of uncertainty and constitutional experiments since 1848 and settled the final form of the Habsburg Empire until its break-up in 1918. The dualist system has been severely criticised by historians for failing to solve the internal problems of the Monarchy, especially the problem of Slav nationalism (**10, 21**). Even at the time critics in Vienna dubbed the new system an 'Empire under notice' (**17**).

Before we make any judgement on the Compromise it is necessary to ask under what circumstances it was created. The Monarchy had just lost the battle of Sadowa in 1866 and was forced to yield control of the Germanic Confederation to Prussia and abandon the province of Venetia to Italy. The power and prestige of the Habsburg dynasty was at its lowest ebb and the outlook was bleak. Franz Joseph was intent on restoring the Monarchy's position as a great power and he sought revenge against Prussia. This could only be achieved by winning over the Hungarians through compromises. The events of 1866–67 illustrate how closely foreign and domestic affairs were interwoven in the Habsburg Monarchy. In the words of Louis Eisenmann, 'modern dualism owes its origin to Sadowa' (**6**).

The man called by Franz Joseph to carry out the internal reorganisation of the monarchy was Baron Beust, a former prime minister of Saxony and bitter opponent of Bismarck's Prussia. But even more important were the statesmen on the Hungarian side. After the defeat at Sadowa the Emperor invited Francis Deák, the leader of the moderate Magyar compromise party, to Vienna and asked him what conditions he would demand to come to a settlement with Austria. His celebrated answer was, 'no more after Sadowa than before' (**16**). Thus encouraged, Franz Joseph restored the Hungarian constitution in February 1867 and authorised the formation of a ministry responsible to the Hungarian parliament. In June Franz Joseph, already Emperor of Austria, was crowned King of Hungary in the most colourful spectacle ever witnessed in Budapest.

The Compromise was a unique constitutional creation. The two independent states were not fully sovereign, as would be the case in a confederation nor was there a state above them, as would be the case in a federation. But they did share a common ruler and were joined together by more than a personal union (**12**). Each half of the Monarchy was completely independent of the other, except for the army, a common ministry of foreign affairs, and the financing of these two activities. Each half had its own prime minister, responsible to Franz Joseph, as King of Hungary and Emperor of Austria. The three common ministries – defence, foreign affairs and joint finances – were appointed by the Emperor, but they were responsible to two bodies, called Delegations, chosen from the Upper and Lower Houses of each parliament. The odd thing about the Delegations was that they met separately in Vienna and Budapest and only communicated to each other in writing.

The basic idea behind the Compromise was the joining together of two sovereign states in a real union (**11**). The two states were in a sense bonded to one another. The Hungarian, Deák, said: 'for us Austria's existence is just as necessary as our existence is for Austria' (**22**). It was not easy for the Austrians suddenly to accept Hungary as an equal partner, when formerly she had been regarded as a mere province of the Empire. But it cannot be denied that the Compromise transformed Hungary from a smouldering antagonist of the Monarchy in the years 1850–66 into a satisfied partner, and thereby strengthened the great-power position of the Habsburgs in Europe (**9, 70**). Without the addition of Hungary the Monarchy could not have faced Russia in the Balkans, and the Slav peoples within it (one half of the total population) might have been drawn irresistibly to the call of Pan-Slavism. As it was, the Habsburg Monarchy recovered its position in Europe, tied itself diplomatically to Germany in 1879 and was given the chance to evolve peacefully over the next fifty years (**11, 12, 15**). The Compromise with Hungary and its foreign-policy corollary, the alliance with Germany twelve years later, determined the shape of domestic and foreign affairs in the Habsburg Monarchy until its collapse in 1918 (**19**).

In domestic affairs the price which Austria had to pay for the Compromise was the complete abandonment of Hungary to the minority Magyar ruling class. The Magyars interpreted the Compromise as an assertion of their traditional constitutional liberties and privileges, rooted in the Pragmatic Sanction of 1713. This interpretation assumed that Hungary was not a multi-national state, but a Magyar national state. Furthermore, the Hungarian interpretation called for a constitutional government in Austria and insisted that Austria, like Hungary, should be a unitary state, not a federal structure. In other words, Magyar predominance in Hungary carried with it, as a corollary, German-speaking predominance in Austria (**13**). All attempts to reform the Austrian half of the Monarchy foundered on the rock of dualism. The reason for this is that 'reform' implied giving a measure of power to the non-Germans and this was something which the German-speakers were not prepared to do. In the words of the Austrian historian, Heinrich Benedikt, 'the Compromise suffered from a chronic illness, whereby the patient lived forever, but could never get well' (**1**).

The greatest shortcoming of the Compromise was its failure to do anything about the non-Magyar and non-German national groups which lived in both halves of the Monarchy and made up over 50 per cent of the population. The Czechs were the national group within Austria who felt most bitterly disappointed by the Compromise because they believed themselves equal in political status to the Hungarians and yet were excluded from power. Their leader, Palacký, had prophesied in 1865: 'the day of the proclamation of the dualism will become with an unavoidable necessity at the same time the birthday of Pan-Slavism in its least desirable form (**10**). Five other national groups – Croats, Germans, Rumanians, Ruthenians and Serbs – lived in both parts of the Monarchy, but any attempt to offer them autonomy was ruled out by the Compromise. The Compromise was in fact concluded between Franz Joseph and the Magyar ruling class and it was accepted reluctantly by the middle-class, German-speaking liberals in Austria. One such liberal, the historian, Joseph Redlich, declared that the institutions created by the 1867 agreement operated like an 'iron frame' which cramped the peoples and classes seeking political recognition (**8**).

Part Two: Domestic Affairs

3 The Nationality Question

> A Great Power can endure without difficulty one Ireland, as England did, even three, as imperial Germany did (Poland, Alsace, Schleswig). Different is the case when a Great Power is composed of nothing else but Irelands, as was almost the history of Austro-Hungary ... (R. Kjellen, quoted in Jászi, (**10**).)

The nationality question dwarfed all other problems in the Habsburg Monarchy and the failure to solve it ultimately caused its downfall in 1918 (**13**). In an age which saw the triumph of the nation-state, a multinational empire was bound to face enormous pressures; indeed, many commentators have claimed that for this reason it was foredoomed to failure (**21**, **22**). The principle of national self-determination reached its apogee in the Versailles Settlement of 1919 and this principle was clearly incompatible with the continued existence of the Habsburg Empire. Still, the nationality struggle must be seen in its contemporary context, not through the distorting lens of historical hindsight. Detailed studies of the problem show that no general guide can be applied to the nationality struggles. Each national group was at a different stage of political, economic and cultural development from the rest and therefore had problems peculiar to it alone (**11**). Two common assumptions about the national groups within the Empire need to be questioned: first, that each nationality believed it could find freedom only outside the Monarchy; second, that all the nationalities were engaged in a struggle against the Habsburg Monarchy rather than amongst each other (**23**).

The very concept of nationality raises difficult problems for the historian. In western Europe the nation has always been closely associated with a territorial unit, the state. In eastern Europe, by contrast, the nation was a personal concept, a blood-tie which existed irrespective of where a person lived (**74**). For a complex set of reasons, the state, composed of a single nationality, was slow to develop in eastern Europe and therefore the two terms, state and nation, never became identical, as they did in western Europe.

Instead of the nation-state, 'historico-political entities', or multinational states, evolved in eastern Europe (**11**). These states (e.g., the Czech Crownlands, the Kingdom of Hungary and the Kingdom of Croatia) were concerned to preserve their ancient rights and privileges. From the middle of the nineteenth century, however, the authority and legitimacy of the older multinational units began to be challenged by the personal concept of nationality based on ethnicity, culture and language and drawing on a broader mass appeal.

There were eleven recognised national groups in the Austro-Hungarian Empire [**doc. 1**]. Since the Empire developed out of a union of historico-political units, not ethnic ones, it is logical to classify the national groups according to their historical tradition. The most famous classification along these lines was made by Otto Bauer, the Austrian Marxist leader. He named the 'historic' nations as those with an independent national political history and a nobility and bourgeoisie, who had created a national culture by the early nineteenth century: the Germans, Magyars, Poles, Italians and Croats (**86**). Nations 'without history', i.e. without an independent political history, included the Czechs, Slovaks, Serbs, Slovenes, Ruthenians and Rumanians. The only category of Bauer's which has been disputed is that of the Czechs, whom most modern scholars would place among the 'historic' nations (**11**).

The Germans

As we have seen, the Compromise of 1867 left the Germans and Magyars in political control of the Austrian and Hungarian halves of the Empire respectively. But numerically the Germans and Magyars together formed slightly less than half of the total population of the Empire. In the western, or Austrian, half of the Empire the Germans numbered just under 10 million people out of a total population of almost 28 million in 1910. At 35 per cent of the population the Germans did not constitute a majority; but it would be inaccurate to describe them as a minority, for no other nationality made up more than half of the population [**doc. 1**]. The Germans, however, were the leading national group in the Empire and exercised an influence out of all proportion to their numbers. Not only was the dynasty itself German in origin, but the modern centralised administration built up from the time of Maria Theresa was thoroughly German in character.

It is important to understand that the predominance of the Germans stemmed not from any nationalist claims, but from the cultural and historical role played by the group. They were the true *Staatsvolk* of the Empire who dominated most of the pro-Habsburg institutions (**84**). The official language of the Empire was German and the civil servants were overwhelmingly German, though their allegiance was to the dynasty. Hermann Bahr, the Viennese critic, called the Austro-German officials 'a new race', loyal to the Emperor Franz Joseph alone (**81**). The army was probably the most pro-Habsburg institution in the Empire, but no less than 78 per cent of the commissioned officers were Austro-German (**19**). Not only was the cultural life of Vienna almost exclusively German, but the capitalist class, the Catholic hierarchy and the press were also the preserve of the Austro-Germans (**84**).

The political problem for Austro-Germans after 1867 was how to retain the German character of the Monarchy with only one-third of the population. The German Liberal Party believed in a centralised state, which in effect meant a German-controlled state, and it successfully dominated Austrian governments until 1879. After this date it never regained power. Three great anti-Liberal German parties sprang up in the 1880s and played a major role in the Empire until its end. The Pan-Germans looked beyond Austria to Bismarck's Germany and stood for a purely nationalist union of all German-speaking peoples. The Christian Social Party, under the renowned Viennese demagogue, Karl Lueger, sought to unite the various nationalities around the dynasty. The third German-dominated party was the Social Democrats, who organized the working class under a banner of international solidarity and came close to making a major contribution towards a solution of the nationality question (see chapter 5).

The history of the last fifty years of the Habsburg Monarchy is to a large extent the history of the failure of the German element to retain its privileged position in an age of democracy and nationalism. The Germans were predominant as both Liberals and anti-Liberals, capitalists and anti-capitalists. But the one group they could not dominate was the Slavs, who made up about 65 per cent of the Cisleithanian (i.e., Austrian) half of the Empire. The Slavs tolerated the privileged position of the Germans so long as it rested on their political and cultural superiority. But once the Germans were viewed as just another national group their days were numbered (**69**).

The Czechs

The Czechs, with a population of 6.5 million, or 12.6 per cent of the total population of Austria, formed the third strongest ethnic group in the Monarchy [**doc. 2**]. They inhabited the ancient, formerly independent, lands of the Crown of St Wenceslas: Bohemia, Moravia and Austrian Silesia. Unlike all the other Slav peoples (with the exception of the Croats and Slovenes) the Czechs lived entirely within the boundaries of the Empire, a fact which is crucial to an understanding of their attitudes towards it. The Czechs had neither irredentist aims, nor did they wish for complete independence; rather, they sought to achieve some form of autonomy within the Empire.

The Czech–German rivalry in Bohemia occupies a special place in the history of the Habsburg Empire, for it was here that the 'technique, psychology and procedure' of the national struggle were fully developed (**12**). In Bohemia roughly two-fifths of the people were Germans, three-fifths Czech [**doc. 2**]. The Germans' traditional supremacy in the area came under threat in the late nineteenth century, when the Czechs experienced a remarkable economic and cultural resurgence. Alone of all the lands in the Monarchy, the national struggle in Bohemia (and Moravia) between Czechs and Germans was conducted by two developed national bourgeoisies (**15**). Nor was it possible to confine the struggle to the Czech Crownlands; behind the Germans in Bohemia stood the Germans in the rest of Austria, as well as those in the German Empire. The Czechs for their part were able to link their cause with that of the other Slavs in the Empire, and occasionally even beyond, to Russia.

The Czechs were profoundly disappointed by the 1867 Compromise, for as the great Czech nationalist, Palacký, warned, it meant the handing over of the Slavs to the mercies of the Austro-Germans on one side of the Leitha (the river dividing Austria from Hungary) and to the Hungarians on the other (**83**). The Czechs, like the Hungarians, had been brought into the Habsburg Monarchy in 1526 and therefore wanted to be recognised as their equals. The first and last attempt to meet the Czech demands for autonomy came in 1871 with Count Hohenwart's ill-fated plan to turn the dualistic Empire into a federal state. The reasons for the failure of the scheme will be examined in chapter 5, but the Czechs never again trusted the dynasty and became increasingly hostile towards it.

From the late 1870s the Czech–German struggle focussed on the issue of language in the administration and in the schools. The

Czechs wanted the equality of all languages in public life and the right of instruction in their own language in schools, even in urban, German-dominated districts of Bohemia (**64**). The Germans successfully resisted these demands, but with each passing decade it became more difficult for them to dismiss the Czechs as a people of 'peasants and servants' (**23**). After all, Bohemia was the most important industrial land of the Empire and a powerful Czech middle class had emerged and set up many national societies, their own bank in 1868, theatre in 1881 and university in 1882 (**77**). Prague, which had been an almost purely German city until the middle of the nineteenth century, was only 6 per cent German by 1910. Politically the new situation was reflected by the appearance in the late 1880s of the 'Young Czechs', a radical, democratic party, not prepared to accept the old German predominance (**82**). The national conflict between Czechs and Germans, in Bohemia and Vienna, continued unabated until 1914 and did much to poison the political atmosphere of the Empire and make parliamentary government unworkable (**64**, **72**, **79**).

The Poles and Ruthenians

The Poles formed the fourth largest national group in the Empire. In 1910 they numbered 4.9 million, or 17.8 per cent of the population of the Cisleithanian half of the Empire, most of them living in the province of Galicia [**doc.1**]. The Poles were more loosely connected with the national problems of the Empire than any other nationality (**23**). They were the youngest national group (Galicia had been acquired only in 1772) and geographically the most remote. The Crownlands of Galicia and Bukovina lay beyond the Carpathian Mountains on the north-eastern fringe of the Empire, far from the Danube basin. The Poles' political position was also different. Unlike the Czechs, Slovaks, Magyars and Croats, all Poles did not live within the Empire; nor did they possess their own national state, as did the Italians, Serbs and Rumanians. The independent state of Poland had been wiped off the map of Europe by three partitions in the late eighteenth century. But the Poles had already had such a well-developed national culture and tradition of independent statehood that they had no need artificially to revive their sense of nationalism in the nineteenth century (**11**).

In the first half of the nineteenth century the Poles were one of the most revolutionary groups in the Empire, but after 1867 their position changed dramatically. The Compromise with Hungary, which alienated the Czechs and Croats, gave the Poles their opportunity. The Austrian government needed the Poles to make up a parliamentary majority in Vienna and therefore it made wide-ranging concessions to the ruling Polish Conservative Party in Galicia. In effect, the Poles won almost complete autonomy in Galicia: Polish was recognised as the official language, Germanisation in the schools was ended, the two universities of Cracow and Lvóy were Polonised and the whole province became a centre of Polish culture. The Poles, led by their upper-class Conservative Party, had become 'the strongest pillar of the Austrian Governmental system' (**11**). They provided the central government with many ministers, including the prime ministers Potocki (1870–71) and Badeni (1895–97) and the foreign minister Goluchowski (1895–1906). In contrast to the position of the Poles living in the German and Russian Empires, the Austrian Poles enjoyed relative liberty and independence (**80**). Of course, they still dreamt of a future unified Polish state, but the ruling nobility, at any rate, remained content with their constitutional position within the Dual Monarchy (**23**).

The Poles, far from being a suppressed nationality, were themselves the ruling group in Galicia. Only three-fifths of the Galician population was Polish; the other two-fifths was Ruthenian and in the eastern half of the province the latter formed the majority (**11**). The Ruthenians belonged to the same ethnic group as the Ukrainians in Russia, but were separated from them by their adherence to the hybrid, Latin/Greek Uniat church. They numbered about 4 million people before 1914, divided among the two Austrian provinces of Galicia (3,380,000) and Bukovina (300,000) and the Kingdom of Hungary (470,000) (**76**).

The Ruthenians were socially the most backward group in the Empire and although they had become aware of their national identity in the early nineteenth century, after 1867 those living in Galicia fell under the rule of the Polish aristocracy and upper bourgeoisie, where they endured a fate similar to the non-Magyar nationalities of Hungary. The provincial diet, the two universities and even secondary education were dominated by the Polish ruling class. The Ruthenians, who were mainly peasants, responded by building a democratically oriented nationalist movement. The social division between Poles and Ruthenians suited the central government in Vienna, for it meant that a united anti-Habsburg policy was out of the question.

Although the Ruthenians had a long tradition of loyalty to the Habsburg Empire – they were known as the 'Tyrolians of the East' –

their subjection to Polish rule in Galicia changed their orientation (**10**). The 'Old' Ruthenians, conservative in outlook and dominated by the clergy, gave way to the 'Young' Ruthenians in the 1880s and 1890s, who sought union with the 30 million Ukrainians living in Tsarist Russia. After 1900 Poles and Ruthenians frequently clashed over educational and electoral issues. With the introduction of universal suffrage in the Cisleithanian half of the Monarchy in 1907 the Ruthenians finally gained a voice in the parliament (though still not in proportion to their numbers) and in 1914 they became partners with the Poles in the provincial government of Galicia (**76**). The Ruthenians never developed a full irredentist movement, but there can be no doubt that the concessions made to Polish rule in Galicia by the central government alienated the Ruthenian peasantry from the Empire. Like the Czechs and South Slavs, the Ruthenians were casualties of the dualist system.

The one territory where a satisfactory solution to the nationality question was reached was Bukovina in the far north-eastern corner of the Empire. Bukovina was the most heterogeneous of the Austrian Crownlands, a land with no absolute national majority, though Ruthenians made up 38 per cent of the population (**10**). In 1910 a new constitution and franchise law gave personal autonomy to the six nationalities of the province. This constitution has been called the 'most satisfactory solution' ever arrived at in Austria, but it was probably only possible because no single national group predominated (**11**).

The Slovenes and Italians

The Slovenes were the largest South Slav group within the Austrian half of the Monarchy, numbering 1.25 million, or 4.4 per cent of the population (**85**). Although they all lived inside Austria proper, they were scattered in six different Crownlands – Carinthia, Styria, Carniola, Gorizia, Istria and Trieste – and formed a majority of the population only in Carniola and Gorizia. The Slovenes were a non-historic people in Bauer's sense of the term; indeed, before the nineteenth century they even lacked a literature in their own language. As Catholics the Slovenes were loyal to the Habsburg Monarchy, but as peasants they were subject to the rule of the towns, under either German or Italian control. The most that Slovenes could hope for from the dynasty in the decades after 1867 was an extension of the use of their own language in the schools and the administration. But even such modest demands led to fierce opposition, mainly from German nationalists; the Windischgrätz cabinet, for example, fell in 1895 over an attempt to set up a Slovene high school in addition to the existing German high school in the town of Cilli in Styria, where the majority of the population was Slovene (**11**). In the years before 1914 some radical anti-Habsburg parties emerged, but on the whole the Slovenes favoured a form of autonomy within the Empire such as the trialist scheme put forward by the Croats in the late 1890s (**85**).

The Italians, with a population of 770,000 in 1910, formed the smallest national group in the Empire [**doc. 1**]. The two Italian-speaking areas were the South Tyrol and the Adriatic Littoral, comprised of three provinces, Gorizia–Gradisca, Trieste and Istria. The existence of the newly unified Italy after 1861 created a focal point of attraction for Italians under Austrian rule and there were frequent calls for union with Italy. But the sentiment of irredentism within the Italian provinces has probably been exaggerated (**10**, **61**). After all, the problems in the South Tyrol and the Littoral were quite different. In the South Tyrol the Italians sought their own assembly, in order to be free from Austro-German domination in Innsbruck. In the Littoral the Italians were outnumbered by the Slavs by almost two to one and there they sought to uphold their privileged positions of control in the cities and the government. In fact, the Italian problem was less a conventional Austrian national problem than a territorial/foreign-policy problem. On the whole, the Italians were a favoured, not an oppressed, nation within the Empire; especially after the franchise reform of 1907 they had more representatives in relation to their numbers than any other national group (**11**). As it turned out, the possession of the 'unredeemed' territories became the price that Italy could demand for becoming an ally. When the Entente powers promised Italy the South Tyrol and the Littoral by the Treaty of London in 1915, a crushing blow was dealt to the Habsburg Empire (**61**).

The Magyars

The Transleithanian half of the Empire, established in 1867, was divided into Hungary proper and Croatia–Slavonia. The main national group living within these lands was the Magyars, who, at nearly 10 million, constituted 48 per cent of the total population of Hungary (excluding Croatia–Slavonia) [**doc. 1**]. The political, economic and cultural hegemony of the Magyars in Hungary had no counterpart in the Austrian half of the Empire. In the Hungarian parliament of 1910, for example, Magyars occupied 405 seats, the Rumanians had 5 and the Slovaks had 3 (**11**). The Magyars totally dominated both the business and professional worlds: they owned 97 per cent of the joint-stock companies and supplied 95 per cent of state officials, 87 per cent of lawyers and over 92 per cent of all high-school and university teachers (**15**).

The nationality problem in Hungary developed in a radically different way from that in Austria. The Nationalities Law drafted by the famous Hungarian Liberal, Baron Eötvös in 1868, recognised the rights of the languages of the various non-Magyar nationalities in schools and local government and granted them equality of status with the Magyars. It was the opinion of twentieth-century scholars of Hungary, such as R.W. Seton-Watson and Oscar Jászi, that this law could have provided the basis for transforming all non-Magyars into loyal citizens of the Hungarian state. But it was never put into effect, for Magyar supremacy won the day. What Louis Kossuth said in 1848 held with even more force after 1867: 'There were many nationalities in Hungary, but only one nation, the Magyars' (**10**). The Magyar outlook was essentially feudal and rested on the power of the landlord class. This class, in alliance with the smaller landed gentry and with the support of a growing business class, pursued a policy of political, economic and cultural discrimination against the non-Magyar nationalities, which had no contemporary parallel.

The policy of Magyar supremacy was social, not racial: it aimed not at the extinction or expulsion of non-Magyars, but at their assimilation (**75**). In other words, if they accepted the Magyar language and culture and abandoned their own nationality and language they would be treated as equals. Those who retained their Slovak, Rumanian, Croatian or Ruthenian nationality and language were fiercely repressed. The schools in particular were used as instruments of Magyarisation. Magyar was the language of instruction in four times as many elementary schools as were non-Magyar languages. At the secondary level Magyar supremacy was even more marked: Slovaks and Ruthenes, for example, had no educational establishments at all above the primary level. As Béla Grünwald said: 'The secondary school is like a big engine which takes in at one end hundreds of Slovak youths who come out at the other end as Magyars' (**10**). Magyarisation also made rapid headway in the towns. Budapest, which had been three-quarters German in 1848, was more than three-quarters Magyar in 1910. Perhaps the most important assimilated group in Hungary was the Jews, who emigrated on a large scale from the east and settled in the towns.

Budapest was one-quarter Jewish by 1900 and was referred to jokingly at the time as 'Judapest' (**15**). In the absence of a strong middle class the Jews came to play a disproportionately large role in the economic and cultural life of the country up to 1918 (**67**).

The Magyarisation process in Hungary continued to gather pace in the two generations after 1867; in Austria, by contrast, the process of Germanisation declined. By the early twentieth century the two halves of the Empire stood radically at odds with each other in their internal nationality policies. As we shall see in chapter 5, all attempts to reform the Dual Monarchy were ultimately stymied by Hungary's refusal to change her policy of Magyarisation (**63**).

The Rumanians and Slovaks

The Rumanians were the largest non-Magyar national group in the Kingdom of Hungary. About 3.25 million lived in the Empire as a whole; 3 million, or 14 per cent, in Hungary proper [**doc. 1**]. They claimed to be a Latin people and had few ethnic and cultural ties with the other national groups in the Empire. Although Rumanians had lived in Transylvania for centuries, they had no independent national history. But they did possess their own cultural identity and desire for autonomy which had been crushed by the Compromise of 1867. Across the Transylvanian borders stood the Kingdom of Rumania, independent since 1859. Irredentist feeling developed amongst Rumanians in Transylvania, but because of Rumania's weakness and her pro-Austrian orientation, she failed to exercise the sort of influence which Italy and Serbia had exerted on Italian and Serbian irredentist sentiment within Austria (**11**).

Hungary's policy of Magyarisation led to the founding of the Rumanian-based National Party in 1881, which demanded autonomy for Transylvania and equality of rights with the Magyars. But true irredentist sentiment took hold among Rumanians in Transylvania only after the failure to introduce a general franchise in Hungary in 1906 and then only among a small, educated section of the population (**60**). Before 1914 the Rumanian nationality problem had become entangled with the foreign policy of the monarchy. The Magyars' oppressive nationalist policy gradually ruined relations with Austria's ally, Rumania, and Franz Ferdinand, among others, was convinced of the need to make concessions to the Rumanians in Transylvania, in order to maintain good relations with Rumania (**10**).

The Slovaks, next to the Rumanians, were the weakest and least privileged national group in the Habsburg Monarchy. They numbered just under 2 million, or 9.4 per cent of the population, and lived entirely within the Kingdom of Hungary [**doc. 1**]. The Slovaks were a peasant people who had lived under Magyar domination for a thousand years and therefore had no independent national history. In the early nineteenth century, however, they rapidly developed a national consciousness and culture and began to forge links with the ethnically related Czechs. The Compromise of 1867 had made the Czechs and Croats into second-class nations. But for the Slovaks it was worse. In the words of a modern historian, 'it augured the tragic destiny of gradual national extinction' (**58**). The Magyars effectively suppressed Slovak culture from the 1870s and the Slovaks could do little to resist the process, but from the 1890s they started to cooperate politically with the Czechs (**11**). The idea of a fully independent Czecho-Slovak state was still not widely envisaged, especially by the Slovaks before 1914; but the experience of Magyar rule since 1867 did much by World War One to convince men such as the future President of Czechoslovakia, Thomas Masaryk (himself a Slovak), of the need for an independent state (**66**).

The Croats and Serbs

The Croats, who made up nearly 9 per cent of the population of Hungary, occupied a position similar to that of the Poles within Austria [**doc. 1**]. Both were privileged – or, more correctly, the least discriminated against – nations in their respective halves of the empire. The Croats were a South Slav people of Roman Catholic affiliation (in contrast to the Greek Orthodox Serbs) who had enjoyed a fair degree of autonomy within their kingdom of Croatia–Slavonia, under Habsburg rule since the eleventh century (**73**). With an independent history and a strong aristocracy, the Croats were the one South Slav group in close touch with the Habsburg Monarchy. Indeed, to them the very word 'Balkan' symbolised 'backwardness, poverty, corruption, violence and injustice' (**68**). It was all the more remarkable then that one of the most loyal national groups in the Empire should have joined with the Serbs and moved into opposition to the dynasty by 1914 (**73**).

In the early nineteenth century Croatia and its capital, Zagreb (Agram), became the centre of the Illyrian movement, an attempt to unify South Slavs culturally against the influence of the Magyars. By the Hungarian-Croatian Compromise (1868) Croatia–Slavonia received autonomy within the Hungarian state, but since the head of the Croatian government, the *banus*, was elected by the Hungarian government, the Magyars imposed an absolutist rule over the Croats The rule of Count Khuen Hédervary (1883–1903), who suppressed the Croat majority, was bitterly resented by the latter and convinced them that their real interests lay in political co-operation with the Serbs (**10**). Croatia now became the centre of the 'Trialism' movement, which envisaged a union of all South Slavs within a federal, tripartite empire under German, Magyar and Croat leadership (**11**). By the first decade of the twentieth century the Croatian national problem had become part of the much larger life-and-death problem of the Habsburg Monarchy – South Slav unity (**141**).

The position of the Serbs was more complicated than that of any other national group because they lived under four different kinds of administration in the Empire (**11**). In 1911 there were approximately 100,000 Serbs in Dalmatia under Austrian administration; 500,000 in Hungary proper; 650,000 in Croatia–Slavonia, the autonomous province within Hungary; and 850,000 in Bosnia–Herzegovina, ruled jointly by Austria and Hungary. Like the Slovenes and Slovaks, but unlike the Croats, the Serbs were a peasant people without a national history within the Empire. But more important for the future of the Monarchy, the Serbs had a focus outside the Empire. In 1878 the independence of Serbia was recognised by the Congress of Berlin and a generation later this small country became the centre of the South Slav independence movement (**78**).

Because of the existence of the independent state of Serbia the internal Serb national problem, like the Italian one, became partly a foreign-policy question. The problem was made even worse by the occupation (1878) and annexation (1908) of Bosnia–Herzegovina, the majority of whose inhabitants were Serbs, who looked to their co-nationals in Serbia for liberation from the Habsburg yoke. The centre of gravity for the Croats had always been within the Empire. But the Serbs living within the Empire increasingly saw their only chance for autonomy as lying in the membership of a Greater Serbian state outside it (**59**). After 1903 Serbia began to lead the struggle for South Slav unity, which in 1914 sparked off World War One.

The Jews

The Jews did not form a very large percentage of the Austro-Hungarian Empire: they made up about 5 per cent of the population in Hungary, just under 5 per cent in Austria (**94**). But two facts stand out as vital to an understanding of the Jewish problem. First, Austrian Jews were concentrated overwhelmingly in Vienna, in contrast to the Jews in Germany, who tended to be scattered in most of the larger towns (**2**). Second, Jews in Vienna came to play a role in certain spheres of imperial life out of all proportion to their numbers. In the second half of the nineteenth century the Jewish population of Lower Austria increased from about 7000 (1857) to 157,000 (1900) (**94**). The vast majority of these Jews came from one province of the Monarchy – Galicia – and settled in one city – Vienna (**91**, **103**). By 1900 Jews made up almost 9 per cent of the population of Vienna [**doc. 12**].

The Jews of Vienna represented every phase of assimilation, from the cosmopolitan, German-educated type to the newly arrived bearded Jews from the East, who wore caftans and spoke Yiddish (**28**). The Jews found many opportunities to rise in commercial and professional life and by the last quarter of the century they were playing a leading role in banking, industry, law, medicine and journalism. Karl Kraus, himself of Jewish origin, was referring to Sigmund Freud and the beginnings of psychoanalysis when he wrote only half in jest: 'The Jews control the press, they control the stock-market, and now they also control the unconscious' (**120**). Most important of all, the terms 'Jew' and 'capitalist' tended to merge together in the public mind, and the class struggle became mixed up with the national and racial struggle (**2**).

In spite of their career successes the Jews in Vienna never really acquired a secure social position; they were never accepted as equals by non-Jews. This affliction ate into their souls and shaped the outlook of all the leading Jews in the Empire, from Sigmund Freud and Franz Kafka to Theodor Herzl and Karl Kraus (**91**, **129**). Gustav Mahler described his own position to his wife as follows: 'I am a thrice homeless man: as a Bohemian among Austrians, as an Austrian among Germans, and as a Jew among the peoples of the whole world' (**116**).

One reason for the uncertainty of the Jews' social standing in Vienna was that they occupied a mid-way position between the status of pariah in the East and complete equality in the West (**2**). There were two extreme and opposite responses to this situation: Zionism and mass conversion. The Zionist movement, founded by Theodor Herzl in 1897 in Vienna, called for an independent state for the Jews (**92, 98, 100**). That solution lay in the future. Meanwhile, conversion was a path chosen mainly by those from the upper stratum of Jewish society. For an aspiring Jew conversion provided what the poet Heine had earlier called 'the admission ticket to European culture' (**116**). It is estimated that about 28,000 conversions took place in Vienna between 1868 and 1929 (**2**).

We shall see in chapter 5 how the fate of Austrian liberalism after 1867 was intertwined with that of the Austrian Jews. The assimilated Jew, brought up on German culture, identified himself with the liberal ideals of parliamentary government, a secular society and *laissez-faire* capitalism. When these ideals came under attack in the 1880s, so too did the Jews. Vienna has been aptly described as 'the cradle of modern political anti-semitism' (**96**). The problem of the Austrian Jews took on worldwide significance in the twentieth century because it was in Vienna that two notorious 'solutions' to it were born – Nazism and Zionism.

4 The Economy

The economic history of the Habsburg Empire has been badly neglected until recently. Most historians have concentrated on foreign affairs and the nationality conflicts within the Dual Monarchy. But in fact, political events are closely connected with economic and social developments and cannot be properly understood in isolation. The national question, for example, was much more than a problem of language among the middle classes. One of its root causes was the gross inequality in the regional distribution of wealth and income. Likewise, the fundamental shift in ideology and politics which took place in the last quarter of the nineteenth century was moulded by economic developments. The collapse of the German Liberal Party, the rise of anti-semitism, and the general trend towards anti-capitalist legislation – as illustrated by the sudden rise of the Viennese demagogue, Karl Lueger, in the 1880s – can only be comprehended in the context of the stock exchange crash in 1873 and the subsequent depression (see chapter 5). These political events, which had such a decisive influence on the destiny of the Habsburg Empire, were a direct consequence of the breakdown of *laissez-faire* capitalism in the 1870s (**52**, **53**).

The 'backwardness' of the economy and the role of the banks

The Habsburg Empire was the only major power (with the possible exception of Russia) to become a modern growth economy and simultaneously suffer political decline (**24**, **47**). It became an industrialised state in the nineteenth century, but did so in a slow, leisurely fashion (**33**). Compared with Germany, the Habsburg economy was certainly backward [**doc. 4**]. In 1911, for example, Austria–Hungary produced less than one-sixth as much steel and one-fifth as much coal as her northern neighbour [**doc. 5**]. The Habsburg economy retained its agricultural character into the twentieth century: in 1910 just over half of the employed population was engaged in agriculture in Austria, about two-thirds in Hungary (**27**, **47**).

The Danube River basin is not a natural economic entity. Galicia and Bukovina were cut off from the main Habsburg domains by the Carpathian Mountains; Trieste and Fiume, the only ports, were not natural outlets for the Empire; Bohemia, the richest industrial province, had its outlet on the Elbe River leading to the North Sea. In spite of these geographical barriers, the Empire achieved a certain internal balance between the predominantly agricultural Hungary and the more industrialised Austria. Following the establishment of the Austria–Hungary customs union in 1850, which created a huge free – trade area, each country became the main trading partner of the other; in 1901, 34 per cent of Austria's exports went to Hungary, while 72 per cent of Hungary's exports went to Austria (**63, 65, 36**).

In his study, *Economic Backwardness in Historical Perspective*, Alexander Gerschenkron put forward the hypothesis that the more backward an economy is, the more it must rely on banks and the state for the capital necessary for industrialisation (**40**). Austria occupied a middle position in the scale of backwardness, and private capital was insufficient to achieve 'take-off'. Thus, 'Austria's economic history is to a large extent, bank history' (**49**). In fact, Austria experienced no 'take-off' or 'spurt' towards industrialisation such as occurred in Germany and Britain. Instead, under the impetus of the banks, Austria grew at a slow, but steady pace over a period of time which can be divided into three distinct phases: 1867–73; 1874–96; 1897–1913 [**doc. 3**].

One of the most decisive periods in Austrian economic history were the 'foundation years' (*Gründerzeit*) from 1867 to 1873. During this time no fewer than 1005 new joint-stock companies were created, almost two-thirds of them in industry (**49**). Most impressive of all was the four-fold increase in the number of steam engines built since 1863 and the doubling of coal output, both indicators of industrial progress (**24**). But the basis of the 'foundation years' was the large Vienna banks (**54**). In the early nineteenth century the capital market in Austria was poorly developed, but with the creation of the Rothschild-controlled Creditanstalt in 1855, the situation changed. The Creditanstalt, with the enormous sum of 60 million guilders in share capital, was modelled on the French crédit-mobilier banks, which combined investment banking with regular commercial banking. Other banks of a similar nature sprang up and there followed a great increase in short-term credit and large-scale financial involvement in industrial activities. For the first time, many industrial shares were sold on the Bourse, and from 1868 to 1873 a great 'fever' of speculation took place. This led to the creation of firms which existed only on paper: the end result was the great crash of 1873 and the subsequent depression (**56**).

The crash of 1873 marked a turning point in the economic, social and political life of the Habsburg Empire (**52**). As we shall see in chapter 5, it signalled an ideological turning point in the history of the Empire: anti-liberal, anti-semitic and anti-capitalist ideas took deep root in the last quarter of the nineteenth century (**53**) as the liberal parties were made the scapegoats of the slump. The crash revealed corruption in leading industrial and political circles and did much to discredit economic liberalism in general. The morality of the 'foundation years' was summed up by the Galician railway director, Ofenheim: 'Railways are not built with moral epigrams' (**49**). After 1873 the emphasis shifted towards economic security, as the railways were brought increasingly under public ownership and there was a greater demand for tariffs, cartels and social legislation.

The seven fat years before 1873 were followed by the seven lean years, during which prices, profits and shares fell dramatically. Owing to public reluctance to invest in industrial securities, and a discriminatory tax structure, the number of new joint-stock companies plummeted from 1005 in the years 1867–73 to a mere 43 in the years 1874–80 (**26**). What about the role of the banks? Recent studies have modified Gerschenkron's thesis that the banks devoted themselves to the promotion of industrial activities (**54, 56**). The relationship between the banks and industry can only be understood in the context of the peculiar economic conditions prevailing in Austria after the crash of 1873. The development of joint-stock companies was slow and there was little investment by either the banks or the public in industrial and railway securities. The banks had close ties with industry at this time, but they provided little risk capital; their main link with industry lay in providing short-term credit on current account. Until 1890 the banks played no part in promoting industrial activity or in providing long-term credit. Thereafter, they again became involved in industry – especially electro-technical, machine-building and petroleum – but only with already well-established firms. The keynote of their behaviour was caution. As R.L. Rudolph has put it: 'the great banks appear to have selected plump, juicy firms with favourable prospects, with the difficulties and risks of their early years already completed' (**54**). Austrian banks had certainly established strong ties with industry by the early years of the twentieth century, but their so-called entrepreneurial role belongs more to legend than to reality (**49**).

In the 1880s Austrian industry entered a new phase. Pig-iron production in 1881 had already surpassed the level of 1873, and ten years later output had more than doubled (**23**). From the 1890s there was a steady expansion in several key industries, such as mining, sugar, petroleum, chemicals, electrics and textiles. On the basis of assets held by financial institutions, it has been estimated that the economy grew at a steady rate of 5.1 per cent from 1873 to 1913 (**44**). The pace of industrialisation in Austria resembled that of France, more than of Germany or Britain (**33**).

The emergence of an industrialised economy was bound to have a great impact on the multi-national Habsburg Empire. But it is not entirely clear whether industrialisation reduced or increased the gap between the advanced and underdeveloped provinces of the Empire. In one sphere of the economy – finance – the different regions were brought together into a coherent unit under the control of the Viennese banks (**43**). As we have seen, the banks played a leading role in the cartels and hence were able to control the progress and allocation of industry within the Empire. But their policy was to preserve the existing economic structure of the monarchy. To quote Oscar Jászi:

> When the ruling 'big banks' established their cartels, they took care that inside of the customs union no new enterprise should be created which could rival their plants. And as their more important industries were originally located in the Alpine and Sudeten territories, their cartel policy damaged in the first place the eastern, middle and southern parts of the monarchy, the agrarian population of which was as yet unable to develop a national industry. ... This narrow-minded monopolistic cartel policy of the Austro-German finance capital and of certain Hungarian groups connected with it controlled almost all branches of industry. It was an economic tyranny which hindered progress in the Hungarian, Slav, and Rumanian territories of the Monarchy, and which thereby obstructed the well-being of the population (**10**).

It must be remembered, however, that capital for investment in industry had never been forthcoming in Austria or Hungary. Furthermore, at least in the decade before the war, there seems to have been a fairly uniform rate of industrial development in all parts of the Empire (**45**).

The position of Hungary in the dual economy

The position of Hungary within the Empire has been the subject of much debate among economic historians (**34,35, 63**). Did Hungary occupy a dominant position in the economic life of the Monarchy, or was she a 'dependent economy' (**62**)? Hungary remained an over-whelmingly agricultural economy and presented the classic example, in Europe at least, of the latifundia system. According to statistics compiled in 1895, just under 4000 landowners (representing 0.16 per cent of all landowners) owned estates of over 1420 acres, so that this small group possessed 33 per cent of the total farming area in the country (**51**). At the other end of the scale, over 1.25 million peasants held land of less than 9 acres (amounting to 6 per cent of the cultivated area), while almost 2 million were landless (**37**). The spread of railways after 1867 opened new markets for grain, and the landowners' response was to increase the arable land at the expense of pasture. During the next 50 years the latifundia actually doubled their share of the total landed property, mostly at the expense of the gentry, while small-holdings remained constant. It would be wrong to assume, as some writers have done, that the large-estate system stifled agricultural output and productivity [**doc. 6**]. In fact, output per worker increased by 15 per cent per annum, from 1870 to 1913 (**38**). Still, Hungarian wheat became less competitive on the world market after 1890 and by 1913 less than 1 per cent of Hungary's wheat exports went outside the Empire. The landowners used their political power to raise the tariff walls and ensure the continuation of the latifundia system (**37**).

With the abolition of serfdom in 1848 a peasant bourgeoisie emerged among the non-Magyar nationalities in Hungary which took over the leadership of the national movements. Lack of adequate land was probably the main reason for the growth of nationalism among these groups. In the Transleithanian half of the Empire the Magyars made up just under 50 per cent of the population in 1910, but they owned 91 per cent of all large estates over 1400 acres (**62**). The social conflicts between rich and poor in the agricultural areas were essentially conflicts between Magyar landlords and impoverished Slovaks, Rumanians, Ruthenians, Serbs and Croats. Industrialisation was also a major factor in the development of nationalism, for most of the industrial concerns were in the hands of Hungarian or Austrian capitalists. In Transylvania, for example, only 2.9 per cent of the capital invested in industrial enterprises was Rumanian (**51**). By the end of the nineteenth century the non-Magyar national movements had won support from the masses because class grievances coincided so closely with national oppression (**34**).

Hungarian historians have pointed out that under the dualist system the structure of Hungarian industry remained backward (**62,51**). Food processing was the leading industry, but textile manufacturing remained underdeveloped, even by eastern European standards. The Hungarian economy as a whole retained its agrarian character, with 60 per cent of the population working in agriculture and only 18 per cent in industry in 1913. On the other hand, in spite of the customs union, Hungary, under the spur of foreign capital and government subsidies, began to industrialise quite rapidly at the end of the nineteenth century. The number of workers in the manufacturing and mining industries rose from about 156,000 in 1890 to about 563,000 in 1913 (**51**). It has been estimated that the overall real growth in net production in Hungary between 1850 and 1913 was 500 per cent, compared with 400 per cent for Austria (**62**). Hungary may have had a backward industrial and class structure, but she was developing at a faster rate than Austria and on balance probably gained more than she lost economically from the dualist system.

Economic progress and the nationality question in Austria

Within the Austrian half of the Empire the centre of industry was located in the Czech Crownlands (Bohemia, Moravia and Silesia). By 1910 almost 40 per cent of the population in the Czech lands was employed in industry and mining, compared to only 23 per cent in the rest of Austria. The Czech lands were the traditional centre of the food-processing (especially sugar beet) and textile industries, but by the end of the nineteenth century the coal-mining, metallurgy and engineering industries had come to be concentrated there. Two ironworks alone in Bohemia and Moravia produced almost one-half of Austria's total pig-iron output in 1911 (**56**)). The bulk of all industry was in the hands of Germans, either from Vienna or living in the Czech lands. But from the 1890s Czech involvement in industry and banking increased rapidly and by 1914 one-quarter of the textile industry was in Czech hands (**24**). During the same period non-German labour migrated into the old German cities, Prague and Pilsen, at such a rate that they soon had Czech majorities. As a result of these developments, Czech nationalist sentiments spread quickly to the working population. Czech socialists, for instance, broke with the notion of class solidarity to demand autonomy for the national groups within the Austrian Social Democratic Party and in 1911 set up their own independent party organisation. Legally, the Czechs may have been just another nationality in the Habsburg

Empire, but in a social and economic sense it is possible to speak of a Czech 'nation' by the first decade of the twentieth century (**50**).

There can be little doubt that one of the root causes of nationality conflicts in both halves of the Empire was the inequality of wealth among the regions [**doc. 7**]. An Austro-German, for example, 'paid on average twice as much in taxes as a Czech, four and half times more than a Pole and seven times more than a southern Slav' (**48**). It was assumed by contemporaries that the spread of industrialisation would lessen the gap between the developed and underdeveloped provinces of the Empire. The difficulty with this assumption is that the time-scale for economic progress did not match the pace of political events: the growth of nationalism ran ahead of economic development. In the annexed provinces of Bosnia–Herzegovina, for example, it was hoped that the loyalty of the people could be gained by raising their standard of living through economic development. A network of railways and roads and some factories were built, but Hungary obstructed a rail link to Dalmatia and in the end not enough was done to stem the tide of South Slav nationalism (**57**). It may even be doubted if any amount of economic growth could have defused Slav nationalism in the two provinces.

The most remarkable attempt to divert attention away from the divisive nationality problem through a plan of economic development was made by Ernest von Koerber, the Austrian prime minister from 1900 to 1904. Koerber had had a long, successful career as a civil servant and he possessed an unrivalled knowledge of the economic problems of the Empire. His long-term goal was to integrate the nationalities of the Cisleithanian half of the Monarchy around a common economic interest. Under the aegis of the state he called for a huge programme of economic development which included a railway link between Bohemia and Trieste, a railway connecting Lemberg in Galicia with Hungary, and the modernisation of the port of Trieste. Koerber's programme eventually foundered through lack of support from the Social Democrats, and also because it ran counter to the orthodox fiscal policies of the finance minister. For a short time Koerber demonstrated that the appeal to economic interests could be stronger than the appeal to national sentiment. The linguistic struggles between Czechs and Germans in the late 1890s had reduced the Austrian parliament to a helpless state of incompetence [**doc. 8**]. Koerber's programme was probably the last chance to restore parliament as a workable institution. Unfortunately, it failed to create an integrating 'ideology of industrialisation' which would shift attention away from the divisive nationality issue (**41**).

As we have seen, the overall performance of the Habsburg economy in the late nineteenth century compares unfavourably with Germany's high-growth economy (**24**). On the eve of World War One, per capita consumption of meat and tobacco was only three-fifths that of Germany, cotton one-half, coffee one-third and coal less than one-quarter (**48**). Foreign trade played a relatively small part in the Monarchy's economy, accounting for only £3 per head of the population, as against £13 in Germany and £22 in the UK [**doc. 4**] (**65**). Most significant of all, more than 3.5 million people emigrated from the Monarchy after 1876, a figure which indicates the failure of Austro-Hungarian agriculture to provide the smaller landholders and the landless with a decent livelihood (**10**).

But to be relatively backward in comparison with the advanced western economies is not the same thing as being stagnant. Austro-Hungarian growth rates were respectable, if not of 'take-off' proportions. Austria's total industrial product increased at an average rate of 3.6 per cent during the years 1880–1913, while Hungary's industrial product increased by about 4.5 per cent (**47**). During the last pre-war decade economic progress was considerable and, according to some estimates, remarkably uniform throughout the Empire (**45**). It is difficult to avoid the suspicion that much comment by historians on the economic performance of Austria-Hungary has been coloured by the knowledge of its political collapse. For contemporary observers its last decade was one of progress and optimism, at least in economic affairs. The British writer, Geoffrey Drage, writing in 1907, before he could have had any inkling of the Monarchy's demise, praised the dualist system as the best 'guarantee of prosperity' for both Austria and Hungary (**5**). The shadow cast by the cloud of political foreboding in the years before 1914 has obscured the solid economic achievement of the Habsburg Empire in its final phase.

5 The Politics of Dualism: 1867–1914

The central government of Cisleithanian Austria from 1867 to 1914 was characterised by frequently changing ministries and clashes with parliament. In that period there were no fewer than 20 prime ministers in Austria and 17 in Hungary, compared to only 5 chancellors in Germany (**12**). An Austrian cabinet was not technically dependent on a vote of confidence in parliament, but the executive branch of government could only function if it was not obstructed by the legislature. Within parliament there were about 40 political parties organised into about 20 parliamentary clubs usually held together by national loyalties (**15**). For this reason issues of social conflict tended to be deflected into nationality debates. Because the parliamentary situation was so confusing we can only refer here to the most important ministries and the problems they confronted.

Liberal predominance: 1867–79

The years 1867 to 1879 were the great period of liberal predominance in domestic Austrian affairs. The German Liberals (i.e., the German-speaking Liberal Party in Austria) were the main upholders of a unitary state (as opposed to a federal state) with a centralised administration. This meant German as the official language, German civil servants and a parliament under a limited franchise in the hands of the German constitutional party. The Liberals were a genuine Habsburg state party, not a narrow nationalist party, but they were unable to appreciate the aspirations of the non-Germans in the Empire (**81**). Adolf Fischhof, the leader of the 1848 revolution in Vienna, prophesied that unless the Habsburg Monarchy transformed itself from a bureaucratic, centralised state into a federal one, which would allow for national autonomy, it was doomed (**17, 65**).

The virtues and shortcomings of the German Liberals can be deduced from the social composition of the party. Drawn from the business and professional classes, they supported *laissez-faire* economic policy, efficient administration, restrictions on the church, improved education and a limited franchise (**84**). Under two aristocratic brothers, Karl Auersperg (prime minister, 1867–68) and Adolf Auersperg (prime minister, 1871–79) the Austrian parliament passed an impressive programme of liberal reforms, similar to that put through by Bismarck in Germany. Anti-clericalism stood at the heart of the programmes: education and marriage were brought into the secular sphere, legal equality of all denominations was recognised and the government won limited control over the legal status of the Catholic Church. The Concordat of 1855, which had given the Church such great legal and educational influence, was revoked in 1870. The Liberals also set up free and compulsory elementary education and brought in a new code of criminal procedure, which included trial by jury. The electoral reform of 1873 strengthened the centralist element in the Austrian constitution by introducing direct parliamentary elections in place of delegations from the provincial diets. But the franchise was not extended (only 5.9 per cent of the population had the vote) and representatives were still chosen by four curias – the great landowners, the chamber of commerce, towns and rural communities (**12, 15, 16**).

In between the two Liberal ministries of the Auersperg brothers, in 1870–71, came the first and last attempt to change the Monarchy in the direction of federalism. The first three years of parliamentary government under the control of the German Liberals had left every non-German nationality dissatisfied. The Czechs and Poles refused even to sit in the Vienna parliament. Prussia's defeat of France in the Franco–Prussian War spelled the end of any hope that Austria might recover her leadership in Germany. Franz Joseph thought, therefore, that the imperial government might be strengthened by giving more scope to the Catholic non-German element in it (**17**). Count Hohenwart, a conservative aristocrat, was appointed prime minister in 1871 and drafted the so-called Fundamental Articles, which would establish a general diet of the three lands of the Bohemian crown, Bohemia, Moravia and Silesia. The Articles, along with a proposed nationality law, would have given the Czechs almost as much autonomy as the Hungarians and put the Czech language on a par with German in the Czech Crownlands (**12**).

Hohenwart's plans would have meant the first step towards a federalisation of the Empire. For this very reason they were not adopted. The main opposition came from the Hungarian prime minister, Count Andrássy, who knew that they would mark the beginning of the end of dualism. The twentieth-century observer may look back with regret at the failure of the Habsburg Monarchy to take the opportunity to transform itself into a gigantic Switzerland. But it must be remembered that federalism was not held in high esteem in Europe at that time. Franz Joseph's biographer, Joseph Redlich, wrote that for the Emperor, 'as for most Europeans of his day, federalism spelt small scale business politically; it spelt weakness' (**17**). After the Hohenwart experiment the Emperor never again allowed anyone even to question the dualist system in his presence (**15**).

The Czechs never trusted the dynasty after 1871. They continued to stay away from the parliament in Vienna, and their leadership passed to the more radical 'Young Czechs' (**83**). The Poles, however, won a large degree of autonomy for Galicia (1873) in return for supporting the Liberals in power and agreeing not to demand any more concessions. Thereafter, they took part in all coalition governments up to 1918 (**80**). The German Liberals returned to power in 1871 and remained until 1878, but their days were numbered. The party split into different factions and lost its hold over the urban middle classes. The crucial event in this process was the economic crisis of 1873, which discredited liberal capitalism and had a devastating effect on the party. The momentous political consequences of the collapse of Austrian liberalism will be discussed in the next section.

The close interaction between foreign and domestic affairs in the Habsburg Empire is illustrated by events in 1878. The Liberals opposed the occupation of Bosnia–Herzegovina in that year because they feared that the acquisition of territories with a Slav population would endanger their leadership in Austria. But they also opposed it on the constitutional grounds that parliament had not been consulted and given its consent. Franz Joseph accepted Auersperg's resignation in 1878 and in the elections of the following year the Liberals were outvoted (they won 140 seats against the 160 of the German, Czech and Polish conservatives). The German Liberals had lost power forever; but more important was the fact that power 'passed away from the people's representatives altogether back into the hands of the Emperor and of his civil servants' (**15**). The end of the Liberals' political hegemony coincided with the decline of the power of parliament itself. Austrian politics moved into a new phase of development (**21**).

The 'iron ring' and the collapse of liberalism: 1879–93

In 1879 Franz Joseph called on his boyhood friend, Count Taaffe, to

Domestic Affairs

form a new government. It was based on the support of German, Czech and Polish conservatives, the so-called 'iron ring' around German liberalism, and it lasted fourteen years – the longest-running government since the fall of Metternich in 1848 (**69**). Reconciliation of national groups and social classes was the aim of Taaffe's policy. The Czechs agreed to re-enter parliament in return for administrative and educational concessions. By 1882 Czech language rights had been extended, the Czech representation in the Bohemian Landtag increased, and the University of Prague divided into two national institutions, German and Czech.

In 1882 a franchise reform was enacted which lowered the property qualification from 10 to 5 guilders, giving the vote to the lower-middle classes in the cities and many peasants in the countryside. Both groups were enemies of big business and at the next election there was a further swing to the right (**15**). In the seven years from 1883 to 1889 Taaffe's cabinet brought in some modest social reforms, including workers' health and accident insurance, restriction of the working day to eleven hours and an inspectorate to enforce these measures (**12**).

Count Taaffe has been perhaps unfairly criticised by historians as a 'sawdust Metternich', who had no policy other than 'muddling through' (**69**). It is true that he allowed Austria to pass from a parliamentary to a bureaucratic form of government, in which most of the ministers were officials, not drawn from parliament. Indeed, Taaffe himself was known as the 'Emperor's minister' (**17**). This system of government, with ministers accountable to the monarch rather than to parliament, was much closer to the German constitution under Bismarck, than to the British one under Gladstone. But within this framework Taaffe made a genuine effort to solve the nationality problem, especially that between Czechs and Germans (**9**, **69**). Indeed, his government was brought down on this issue.

In 1890 Taaffe attempted to diminish the embittered Czech–German rivalry by dividing those Czech provinces in which two or more nationalities lived into administrative districts along ethnic and linguistic lines. Had the plan succeeded it might have set a precedent for further national reforms and eventually transformed the Empire (**9**). The conservative Old Czechs and the Germans had agreed to the reforms, but the more radical Young Czechs won the elections of 1891 (returning 37 deputies against the Old Czechs' 12) and rejected outright Taaffe's plan (**82**). Taaffe then decided to extend the franchise in the hope that the working classes would concentrate on economic and social issues and that the national struggle would fall into abeyance. But his electoral reform bill failed because three parties – the Poles, the Clericals and the Feudals – as well as the German Liberals combined to oppose it and thereby forced Taaffe to resign in 1893.

More important to the ultimate destiny of the Empire than Taaffe's balancing act was the emergence of three mass movements during his time of office which swept the Liberals off the centre of the political stage. Two of the movements – social democracy and Christian socialism – were anti-capitalist, but they cut across the national question and acted as an integrating force on the Monarchy. The third – Pan-Germanism – was an extreme nationalist movement pledged to the idea of union with Germany.

THE SOCIAL DEMOCRATS

The social democratic movement was the closest in spirit to the old Austro-German liberalism. Implicit in its socialism was a strong centralist approach to the nationality problem. Furthermore, like the Liberals, the Socials Democrats justified the existence of Austria as a bulwark against a Russian-inspired pan-Slavism (**11**). The Austrian labour movement originated in the 1848 revolution, but during the next 40 years it was plagued by government repression and internal dissension. A unified Social Democratic Party (SDP) emerged from the Hainfeld Conference of 1889, under the leadership of Victor Adler and in close association with the trade unions (**90**). At the first May Day demonstration of Viennese workers in 1890, Karl Renner, the future Socialist leader, observed that 'something new had appeared on the historical stage, and held prodigious events in store for our generation' (**86**).

The campaign for the extension of the franchise kept the Socialists united up to 1906. In the 1907 elections the SDP won 87 seats and became the largest single party in parliament. Thereafter, the Socialists shifted the emphasis to economic and social reforms and in the process became a reformist party intent on preserving the Austrian state. The SDP was Marxist in outlook, but it was not a revolutionary party [**doc. 12**]. It rejected the dogmatic, materialist outlook of its German counterpart and developed a more open, reformist approach to economic problems (**99**). A number of brilliant thinkers, such as Max Adler, Rudolf Hilferding, Otto Bauer and Karl Renner, published their main works in the decade before 1914, making this period a 'golden age' of Austro-Marxism (**86**). Leon Trotsky, who lived in Vienna from 1907 to 1914 and frequented the Central Café, where the Austro-Marxists met, deplored their lack of revolutionary zeal [**doc. 9**].

One reason why the Austro-Marxists could not take a straight-forward, class-based approach to social and political problems was the existence of the nationality question (**90**). At the Brünner Congress (1899) the SDP called for the transformation of the Habsburg Monarchy into a democratic federation of nationalities. This federal scheme differed from the previous ones, in-so-far as it rested on the principle of ethnic federalism, instead of the historic Crownlands, as the basis of territorial autonomy (**11**). But what is significant about the Brünner programme is that it sought to reconcile the organised working class to the idea of the Austrian Empire. The two leading socialist theorists on the nationality question, Karl Renner and Otto Bauer, wrote influential books calling for the solution of social problems within the context of a multi-national federal state (**86**).

The Austro-Marxists of the SDP were forced to think about the problem of nationalism in a way that no western socialists were obliged to do (**93**). They learned of the destructive power of nationalism from the fierce Czech–German struggles within their own party. For this reason they adopted a pro-Austrian position and in spite of their violent anti-liberal rhetoric they were, in some ways at least, the heirs of the Austro-German Liberals in the early twentieth century (**11**).

THE CHRISTIAN SOCIALS

The second great mass movement to break away from Austrian liberalism was the Christian Social Party, founded by Karl Lueger (1844–1910). Lueger entered municipal politics in the early 1870s and later became Vienna's most popular mayor (1897-1910) (**97**). He began his political career in the Vienna City Council as a Liberal, but soon turned against the monopoly and corruption of the ruling Liberal oligarchy and demanded an extension of the franchise. Lueger brought a new style to urban politics with his direct appeals to the 'little man' (the lower-middle-class shopkeeper and artisan) to make his voice heard in political affairs (**88**).

Lueger entered parliament in the 1880s as a Democrat and soon found in Catholicism an ideology which integrated all the anti-Liberal elements in his politics: democracy, social reform, anti-semitism and loyalty to the dynasty. He brought all these strands together in the Christian Social Party in 1890 (**88**). In the subsequent years, Lueger, known as the 'beautiful Karl' (*der schöne Karl*), captivated the hearts and won the votes of Vienna's lower social strata through his spellbinding oratory and professional political organisation. As Mayor of Vienna he achieved almost legendary fame until his death in 1910. Among the mourners at his funeral was Adolf Hitler: 'When the mighty funeral procession bore the dead mayor from the City Hall towards the Ring, I was among the many hundred thousands looking on at the tragic spectacle. I was profoundly moved' [**doc. 1**].

Partly because of Hitler's known admiration for Lueger's anti-semitic, rabble-rousing techniques the latter has been seen as a proto-fascist intent on destroying the traditional state and rule of law. Recent scholarship has modified this picture of Lueger. His anti-semitism, in contrast to von Schönerer's, was a political weapon not a racial doctrine, as illustrated by his famous phrase, 'who is a Jew is something I determine' (**89**). Hitler himself called it a 'sham' anti-semitism. Furthermore, though it is true that Lueger was the first Austrian politician to mobilise the masses, the core of Christian Social support came from the same small district and ward clubs in Vienna which had earlier supported the Liberals. J.W. Boyer has shown that Lueger's politics were deeply rooted in nineteenth-century traditions and values: 'he sought not the role of a demagogic and authoritarian *Führer*, but rather that of a patrimonial and patriarchal *Vater*' (**88**). From the standpoint of Austrian liberalism, Lueger's Christian Social movement was destructive, but from an imperial perspective it was an integrating force. It cut across the national question and turned the hitherto disenfranchised artisans and shopkeepers into a powerful anti-socialist, anti-capitalist, pro-Habsburg political force (**19**).

THE PAN-GERMANS

The third movement to disrupt Austrian liberalism was the extreme anti-semitic Pan-German party founded by Georg von Schönerer (1842–1921). Von Schönerer was a 'frustrated aristocrat' who carved out a political career for himself by strident appeals to the masses to reject the consensus politics of the bourgeoisie (**97**). He entered parliament in 1873 as a progressive liberal, but soon criticised his colleagues for their indifference to social questions and their failure to combat the growth of Slav nationalism.

Von Schönerer and a group of young left-wing Liberals openly challenged their party in the so-called Linz Programme (1882): this called for closer links with Germany, extension of the franchise and social reform. Behind the scenes von Schönerer's demands were more extreme. He was in close touch with the nationalistic student associations, which called for the break-up of the Slav part of the

Monarchy so that Austria could unite with Bismarck's Germany. In parliament von Schönerer let slip the remark: 'if only we already belonged to the German Empire' (**97**). In the same year he won support from the Viennese artisans by openly attacking the Jews as exploiting capitalists. He won even greater notoriety in 1884 when he led the fight to nationalise the Nordbahn railway, which had been privately financed by the House of Rothschild. Although he lost the campaign, von Schönerer gained wide popular support by presenting the issue as one of 'the Jews versus the people' (**101**).

In parliamentary terms the Pan-Germans were small; they did not become an independent political party until 1885 and then won only five seats. But they succeeded in making anti-semitism a major issue in Austrian politics [**doc. 11**]. As Hannah Arendt has observed, the Jews were the 'state people' *par excellence* in Austria (**97**). In other words, they did not constitute a nationality; their allegiance was to the Emperor and the liberal political system which allowed them to participate quite freely in the affairs of the Empire (**103**). As an extreme German nationalist, von Schönerer opposed all institutions and ideologies which held the Monarchy together. These included Catholicism, socialism, liberalism and monarchism. The Pan-Germans, with their racial ideas and addiction to violence, attacked all imperial institutions and at the same time posed as the purest of patriots.

The end of parliamentary government: 1893–1914

Was parliamentary government in Austria compatible with the growth of nationalism, which set all the parties in opposition to one another? Franz Joseph believed it was not, and the fate of the next two governments under Windischgrätz (1893–95) and Badeni (1895–97) did much to confirm his view (**17**). The national conflict began to play a conspicious role in Austrian politics from this time onwards, and at its heart was the language question in areas of mixed nationality. The Windischgrätz government was made up of a coalition of the parties which had brought down Taaffe. It fell in 1895 on a relatively trivial national issue. The Slovenes had demanded parallel classes in their own language in a German secondary school in the town of Cilli in southern Styria. The demand was met by Plener, the minister of finance, but when his own German National Party in parliament rejected it the coalition was forced to break up (**18**).

The next prime minister was a Pole, Count Badeni, who as

governor of Galicia had acquired a reputation as a strong administrator and non-party man. Badeni successfully introduced a reform of the franchise which added a fifth curia (based on a general franchise) to the four existing curias. The retention of the curia system gave the upper and middle classes a disproportionate strength in parliament and the new curia added 72 representatives to the existing body of 353 (**12**). Badeni needed a parliamentary majority to pass the decennial revision of the Compromise with Hungary. In order to secure it he turned to the Young Czechs, who demanded a settlement of the language conflict between Czechs and Germans in Bohemia and Moravia.

Badeni attempted to settle the problem by issuing two language decrees in 1897, which provided for the conduct of official business in both Czech and German in both provinces. It was further stipulated that no person was to be employed after 1901 in the administrative and judicial services who was not acquainted with both languages (**15**). In other words, Czech was to be put on an equal footing with German. Since most Czech officials also knew German, but few Germans knew Czech, the Germans rejected the proposals as discriminatory. There followed a political explosion in the Vienna parliament. German Liberals and nationalists filibustered against the bill and when standing orders were used to crush their delaying tactics, riots broke out in parliament and spilled into the streets of Vienna, as well as the German towns in Bohemia [**doc. 8**]. Until now the Czechs had been the great masters of parliamentary obstruction, but the *furor Teutonicus* of 1897 went far beyond anything the Czechs had done and forced Franz Joseph to accept Badeni's resignation. The fall of Badeni proved to be a turning point in Austria's history; parliament never really recovered and the Emperor's authority was weakened (**21**). Looking back on the events of 1897 Joseph Redlich declared: 'From this moment the Habsburg realm was doomed' (**17**).

Redlich's statement must not be taken literally. The Empire was far from doomed, but it is true that the Austrian parliament never functioned properly again and legislation could only be passed by emergency decree, the infamous Article 14. The government which succeeded Badeni was made up of permanent civil servants who carried on either without parliament altogether, or by using Article 14. Meanwhile, the Germans and Czechs continued to obstruct parliament, the language ordinances were withdrawn and no solution was found to the problem. In 1900 von Koerber became prime minister. But as we have seen in chapter 4, Koerber failed to overcome the national conflicts by a series of economic projects and he was forced to resign in 1904. It now seemed that Austria could only be ruled by non-parliamentary methods.

Economic reform had failed to deflect attention away from national passions. The last hope now lay in reform of the franchise. Franz Joseph had come to favour the enfranchisement of the working class, not as a desirable end in itself, but because he thought it might save the Monarchy from the corrosive national disputes engaged in by the middle classes (**17**). Under the ministries of Paul von Gautsch (1904–6) and Max von Beck (1906–8) the question of electoral reform was tackled, and in January 1907 the bill introducing direct and universal suffrage (for all males over 24) became law. Austria now had a 'democratic' parliament, but in fact by this time parliament did not rule Austria (**15**). Beck's ministry, half of which was drawn from parliament, half from the civil service, was the last government to have close links with parliament.

The Emperor's expectation that electoral reform would ultimately solve the national conflict proved unfounded. In the subsequent elections of 1907 and 1911 fewer Germans and Poles and more Czechs, Ruthenians and Slovenes were returned to parliament. But more significant was the fact that the vertical stratification by nationality was now crossed horizontally by parties based on social class, such as the Christian Socials and Social Democrats. In 1907, for example, the Social Democrats won 87 seats – 50 Germans, 23 Czechs, 7 Poles, 2 Ruthenes and 5 Italians (**15**). The extension of the franchise had not made Austria an easier country to govern. During the feeble ministry of Baron Bienerth (1908–11) no fewer than 30 parties blocked all constructive measures in parliament and made an election in 1911 necessary. It was one of the most barren periods in Austrian parliamentary history. Joseph Redlich's diary entry for 26 March 1911 referred to the Bienerth ministry as 'A government without plans, without talent, without ideas' (**29**). The last peace-time Prime Minister, Count Stürgkh (1911–16), avoided national issues and frequently resorted to Article 14. Indeed, his use of Article 14 to adjourn parliament in March 1914 deprived the people's representatives of the means to voice their views in the crisis of July 1914 and was to have enormous consequences during the war (**12**).

Austro-Hungarian conflict: 1903–14

We have seen in chapter 3 that Hungary, in spite of the Nationality Law (1868), pursued a policy of Magyarisation in the two generations after 1867. Hungarian politics were dominated by the Magyar gentry who, through the so-called Liberal Party, defended their narrow class and national interests (**15**). Under Prime Minister Kálmán Tisza (1875–90) the Liberal Party upheld both the policy of Magyar supremacy in Hungary and the Compromise with Austria (**75**). After 1890, however, a younger generation of Magyars came to believe that Hungary could stand alone and they denounced the Compromise. Ironically, it was the very economic success which Hungary enjoyed under the joint tariff system of the Compromise with Austria which helped to nurture her national self-confidence (**10**).

In 1894 the body of the famous revolutionary of 1848, Louis Kossuth, was brought home for a public burial, and his son Frances assumed the leadership of the extremist Independence Party. Every ten years there was a dispute between Hungary and Austria over the quota for joint expenditure by the two states (in 1867, 70 per cent was paid by Austria, 30 per cent by Hungary) (**12**). But the real conflict came in the military sphere when Hungary demanded an independent Hungarian militia (the Honvéds) with Magyar as the language of command (**30, 143**). In 1903 Franz Joseph insisted on a 'common and united' army (**17**). A compromise bill was passed, but in the subsequent elections of 1905 the new prime minister, Stephan Tisza, was defeated by Magyar extremists. The latter formed a coalition around the Independence Party and refused to co-operate with the Crown (**15**).

For 36 years Franz Joseph had ignored the fate of the non-Magyar nationalities in Hungary. In Joseph Redlich's words, it was his 'gravest sin' (**17**). Now, because the constitutional basis of dualism was under threat, he had a general franchise bill introduced in the Hungarian parliament in 1905, which would have undermined the whole basis of Magyar supremacy. Universal suffrage was a 'double challenge' to the Magyars, for it threatened both their national and class privileges (**21**). It would have put them in a minority among the other nationalities and it would have placed the gentry in a minority among the Magyar peasants and the urban working class. Franz Joseph's action had its desired effect: the coalition under the lead of the Independence Party withdrew their demand for revision of the Compromise and the franchise bill was dropped.

The constitutional conflict between Austria and Hungary over the Compromise of 1906 revealed what had been dimly perceivable in 1867: that Magyar dominance in Hungary was the most important condition of the dualist system. It is small wonder that by the early years of the twentieth century many people, including the heir to the throne, Franz Ferdinand, were beginning to question how far dualism was compatible with the very preservation of the Habsburg Monarchy (**10, 144**).

6   Vienna – Cultural Centre of the Empire

Vienna enjoyed its greatest period of cultural activity from 1890 to 1918, at exactly the time when the Habsburg Empire was patently failing to solve its domestic and foreign problems. The unwieldy Habsburg constitution was unable to cope with the problems of nationalism, democracy and social change. The consequence was a series of 'affairs' and scandals which periodically rocked the Empire (**108**). The most famous of these were the suicide of Crown Prince Rudolf at Mayerling in 1889; the Cilli affair, the German–Slovene language dispute in Styria, which brought down the government in 1895; the Zagreb trial, in which the historian Heinrich Friedjung had to confess to using false documents in a treason trial in 1909; and the Redl affair, in which the deputy director of Imperial and Royal Army Intelligence was discovered to be a traitor and homosexual and was forced to commit suicide in 1913, so as to preserve the respectability of the army. In each case unpalatable facts had to be suppressed in order to keep up the appearance of order and stability.

Yet at precisely this time in Vienna, Arthur Schnitzler and Hugo von Hofmannsthal were writing plays, Sigmund Freud was practising psychoanalysis, Gustav Mahler and Arnold Schoenberg were composing music, Gustav Klimt and Egon Schiele were painting and Karl Kraus was writing satires. Vienna in the early twentieth century was a great forcing-house of artistic and intellectural innovation in at least six different fields: music, literature, art and architecture, psychology, philosophy and economics (**106, 109**). It is an open question whether there is any causal connection between the backward political situation in Austria–Hungary and the creative, cultural outburst of Vienna. But there can be no doubt that the golden age of Viennese culture co-existed with an iron age of imperial politics.

The cultural rebellion against liberalism

The great flowering of Viennese culture in the late nineteenth century must be seen in the context of the same crisis of liberalism which unleashed the anti-liberal, mass political movements. At the risk of oversimplifying a complex subject it is possible to detect three separate phases of cultural rebellion against liberalism: the 1870s, the 1890s and the post–1900 period.

THE 1870s
In the 1870s a group of radical students – including Gustav Mahler, Victor Adler and Heinrich Friedjung – formed the 'Pernerstorfer Circle' (named after Engelbert Pernerstorfer, the Socialist parliamentarian) in search of an alternative cultural outlook to the predominantly liberal one (**111**). They took as their starting point the early writings of Nietzsche, especially *The Birth of Tragedy*, which condemned contemporary culture as too rationalistic and fragmented. Nietzsche urged the re-introduction of the 'Dionysian' elements of emotion, feeling and religion into culture. The closest approximation to this was Wagner's music dramas; the group did much to promote Wagnerian ideals after the master's death in 1883. The main political achievement of the Circle was the writing of the Linz Programme (1882), which called for social reforms and the extension of the suffrage and did so much to undermine Austrian liberalism. Thereafter, the members branched off in different directions: Friedjung toyed with Pan-Germanism, Adler founded the Social Democratic Party and Mahler began his career in music (**111**).

The clash of views between the young Wagnerians and the older liberals is beautifully portrayed in some of the stories of Ferdinand von Saar (1833–1906), a conservative writer who saw the new intellectual and social movements as a threat to the old social order. In *Dissonances* (1900), a story set on a country estate, he depicts the clash of ideals between a young, rootless socialist and an older aristocrat and suggests that the new ideas portend an era of endless social conflict (**127**). This theme is taken one step further in the short story, *Die Familie Worel* (1904), which charts the downfall of a family, who, infected by the new social ideas, cut their ties with the local lord, settle in the city and encounter nothing but misery (**128**).

THE 1890s: 'YOUNG VIENNA'
The second wave of rebellion against liberalism began in the 1890s and centred on the literary circle known as 'Young Vienna' (*Jung Wien*). The main writers were Hermann Bahr, Arthur Schnitzler and Hugo von Hofmannstahl (**102**). The distinguishing characteristic of

Young Vienna was their aestheticism, their desire to escape from the world of action and politics and give free rein to their own inner feelings (**97**). As Carl Schorske has pointed out, aestheticism, like the mass political movements of the same period, was part of the larger process of the decay of liberalism. The Young Vienna circle may have been isolated from political life, but they were in close contact with one another, meeting almost daily in one of the hundreds of coffee houses in Vienna [**doc. 13**].

Hermann Bahr and the Young Vienna circle cultivated a form of literary impressionism. Like the impressionist painters in France, they believed that only sense perception could lead to truth and that sense data could be best understood by breaking down the whole into small pieces. In other words, the only thing we can know for sure is our own ideas and sensations, not external reality. The effect in literary terms was a preoccupation with change (and death) and novelty; the fleeting impression became more important than the reality underneath (**109, 110**).

The negative side of the Young Vienna school was its superficiality; the positive side was its willingness to explore the inner feelings. The member of the school who went furthest in this respect was Arthur Schnitzler (1862–1931), whose writings, along with Hofmannstahl's, have survived to the present day. Schnitzler trained as a physician, but soon abandoned this career to become a writer. His early plays, such as *Anatol* (1893) and *Liebelei* (1894), were witty satires on the typical Viennese subject of liaisons between young unmarried girls (*süsse Mädel*) of the lower middle class and elegant young men not yet ready to marry. They reflect the world-weary morality of young dandies and gently expose the hollowness of the codes and conventions which govern his characters' behaviour (**123**). Schnitzler's frank treatment of sex shocked the Viennese, but Freud described the author in 1912 as a 'colleague' in the investigation of the 'underestimated and much-maligned erotic' (**97**).

THE POST – 1900 PERIOD: KRAUS, LOOS AND SCHOENBERG

The third phase of rebellion against liberalism began around 1900 and took the form of a bitter reaction against the impressionism and aestheticism of Young Vienna. Three personalities dominated the movement: Karl Kraus, the satirist, Adolf Loos, the architect, and Arnold Schoenberg, the composer. From 1899 to 1936 Karl Kraus published a satirical fortnightly paper, *The Torch* (*Die Fackel*), in which he attacked the leading writers and artists of the day (**105**). He directed a one-man crusade, not against any particular opinion or ideology, but against loose speech, sentimental pomposity and above all, misuse of language. In the words of Erich Heller 'the tirades of rhetoricians, the pamphlets of politicians, the *feuilletons* of renowned authors are passed through the filter of language, leaving behind mere dregs of folly and residues of false pretence' (**107**). Kraus saw more clearly, perhaps, than any other contemporary Austrian writer how the political corruption of the Habsburg Empire was mirrored in the corrupt use of language (**108**). He called the Empire the 'Research Laboratory for World Destruction'. The very proliferation of ideologies in Austria since 1848 – ranging from Pan-Germanism to socialism and psychoanalysis – was for him a symptom of mental hysteria, a sure sign of a culture in decay (**105**).

The visual counterpart to Kraus's criticism of the literary impressionists was the attack on all forms of decoration and ornamentation by the architect Adolf Loos (**108**). Until the mid-1890s art in Vienna had been dominated by the lavishly decorated realistic paintings of Hans Makart. In 1898 Gustav Klimt led a group of young student artists away from the academy of Makart to form the Secession, which rejected the idea of any fixed views of what art should be [**doc. 13**] (**121**). The architects and designers of the Secession turned their backs on the ornate, neo-Renaissance buildings of the Ringstrasse. The new style was exemplified by the completely unadorned building which Adolf Loos erected in 1910 in the Michaelerplatz, opposite the Imperial Palace. The 'house without eyebrows' (the windows had no lintels) affronted contemporary taste and insulted Emperor Franz Joseph to such an extent that he is reported never to have gazed out of his favourite window again (**115**).

Vienna: the birth of a 'modern' outlook

Kraus, Loos and Schoenberg (like Schnitzler and Freud in their different ways) all looked beyond contemporary taste to the timeless elements in their respective art forms. The immediate object of their attack was the impressionism of Young Vienna. But behind the Young Vienna movement lay the legacy of the baroque. It is a paradox, but an understandable one, that only a city so single-minded in its attempt to maintain beautiful appearances in art could breed a reaction to itself and sow the seeds of a 'modern' outlook. In the words of the cultural historian W.M. Johnston, 'This ability to peel away layers of ornament to expose unvarying realities beneath is turn-of-the century Vienna's most valuable contribution to Western culture' (**110**).

All the certainties in art, politics, culture and society melted in the cultural cauldron which produced such a remarkable flowering of art and thought in Vienna around 1900. The actual collapse of the Empire in 1918 was to a large extent prefigured in the art and literature of the period two decades earlier. As we have seen in chapter 5, the political crisis in late nineteenth-century Austria–Hungary was caused by the bankruptcy of liberalism. The result was the sudden growth of a number of anti-liberal mass movements. In the cultural sphere the consequences of the breakdown of liberalism were no less dramatic.

Traditional liberal culture was founded on the premise of rational man existing within a stable, civic social order. By the 1890s this society was beginning to distintegrate and Vienna's writers and artists turned to the individual in isolation from his social surroundings. Owing mainly to the influence of the café, Vienna's intellectual élite (unlike its counterpart in London, Paris and Berlin) tended to know one another well and to learn from each other's disciplines (**97**). But more important, they felt alienated as a group from political power and this feeling was heightened by the fact that a disproportionate number of artists and writers were Jews. In spite of their cultural achievements Vienna's Jews always considered themselves, to a greater or lesser degree, as outsiders.

In this atmosphere of social and political disintegration the Jewish intelligentsia of Vienna rejected the liberal model of rational man and discovered psychological man, for whom instinct and feeling were more important than reason. Freud's discovery of the subconscious roots of human behaviour was perhaps the most dramatic example of the new orientation. But it was only part of a much larger quest undertaken by his Viennese contemporaries into the inner psyche of man, which has done so much to shape our outlook in the twentieth century.

Part Three: Foreign Affairs

7 The Dual Alliance:1867–1906

1866 was a fateful year for the Habsburg Empire. The disastrous defeat at Sadowa caused not only the establishment of the Dual Monarchy, but also a major re-orientation of foreign policy (**130**). In 1859 Austria had lost her influence in Italy; in 1866 she lost her influence in Germany. What remained? The Balkans. Henceforth the main thrust of Habsburg foreign policy was eastwards into the Balkans (**148**). This was an area where Russia had strong interests and it was here that armed conflict occurred between the two great dynastic empires in 1914. Was Habsburg foreign policy in the Balkans peaceful and defensive, or aggressive and expansionist?

Beust and Andrássy, 1867–79

Austria was diplomatically isolated after Sadowa and needed peace and economic and constitutional reform, so that she could again make her voice heard in European affairs. The man charged with the task of bringing this about was the former foreign minister of Saxony, Baron Ferdinand Beust, whom Franz Joseph appointed as foreign minister in August 1866. Beust was an avowed opponent of Bismarck and his appointment was taken by many as a sign that Austria was intent on a policy of revenge. But such proved not to be the case. The new foreign minister was eager to prevent the four south German states (Bavaria, Würtemberg, Baden and Hesse) from joining the North German Confederation. At the same time he had to avoid becoming too pro-French for fear of alienating the south German states. His position was one of 'neutrality with armament' (**140**). He skilfully manoeuvred between Germany and France and was successful in restoring Austria's influence in German affairs by 1870.

Beust's main problem, however, came not from Germany but from Russia in the Near East. Since the time of Peter the Great Russia had stood as champion of the Slavs under Turkish rule (**142**). Now that Turkey was in decay Austria feared that Russia would become the sole heir to the Ottoman Empire in the Balkans.

She also feared that her own empire, with its large Slav population, was in danger. In 1870 a Pan-Slav Russian general wrote a book, *Opinion on the Eastern Question*, in which he advocated the forceful liberation of the Slavs in Austria–Hungary. It contained the famous sentence: 'The road to Constantinople lies through Vienna' (**130**). Austria was in a weak position – her army had not been reformed since the defeat at Sadowa – and she could not afford to be at odds with both Russia and Prussia.

In the event it was France, not Russia, which thwarted Austria's influence in Germany and endangered her interests in the Near East. Austria was quite prepared to help France gain a peaceful diplomatic victory over Prussia in the Hohenzollern candidature dispute in Spain in 1870. But France rushed headlong to war, the south German states linked up behind Prussia in defence of the national cause, and Austria found herself in a position of uneasy neutrality. Prussia's decisive victory over France at Sedan left the Habsburg Monarchy more isolated than at any time since 1866. Yet Austria's very vulnerability led Beust to make a fresh reappraisal of his foreign policy. In the memorandum written for the Emperor in 1871 he urged Austria to abandon past dreams of becoming a German power and seek a reconciliation with Berlin. Austria needed her strong neighbour as an ally in the struggle against Russia in the Balkans. This was the policy which came to be associated with Andrássy in the 1870s; in fact, it was begun by Beust just before his fall from power in 1871 (**140**).

Beust's successor at the Ballhausplatz (the Austrian Foreign Ministry) was the colourful Magyar aristocrat, Count Julius Andrássy, who directed Habsburg foreign policy from 1871 to 1879. Austria now faced east for the first time in her history (**148**). Russia presented the greatest challenge to Austria, both as a great power and as patron of the Christian Slavs. But Andrássy rejected territorial expansion as a means to meet it; he thought the Hungarian ship of state was already 'overloaded' (**130**). Franz Joseph, likewise, was against increasing the Slav element in the Empire, for he considered the South Slav countries as 'unprofitable' (**17**).

The difficulty with this policy of restraint was that Turkey had only a precarious hold over her Balkan subjects, and should she fail to maintain it, a power vacuum would result. Should Rumania and Serbia become fully independent, for example, they would exercise a powerful attraction over their fellow countrymen within Hungary and Austria respectively. Andrássy successfully kept Russia at arm's length in Rumania (still a vassal state of Turkey) by concluding a commercial treaty with Rumania and by building a Budapest–Bucharest railway in the mid-1870s. Serbia (also a vassal state of Turkey) was a more difficult nut for Austria to crack. Since 1868 the Serbian ruling family of Prince Milan had been pro-Austrian but in the country at large there were strong nationalist and pro-Russian elements. Austria's main fear was that Serbia, under Russian patronage, would absorb the neighbouring provinces of Bosnia and Herzegovina and thus create an independent Great Serbia (**142**). Such a state would become a focal point of attraction for all the South Slavs within the Habsburg Empire (see chapter 9).

The unstable situation in the Balkans made it likely that Austria and Russia would some day come to blows in the area. Austria therefore needed allies. As Britain was too far away and France too weak and isolated, the obvious choice was Germany. Andrássy formed a close relationship with Bismarck and got assurances from him that Berlin would not tolerate an attack by Russia on the Empire. From this position of support Andrássy reached a reconciliation with Russia; by the Schönbrunn Convention (1873) the two countries agreed to uphold the *status quo* in the Near East. Germany joined later in the year to form the Three Emperors' League, a loose association pledged to defend monarchical solidarity against 'the Revolution' (**130**).

The Three Emperors' League received a severe blow in 1875 when Bosnia and Herzegovina rebelled against Turkish rule and sparked off a European crisis which lasted three years. Andrássy was content at first to allow Turkey to crush the rebellion, but the unrest soon spread and in 1876 Serbia and Montenegro declared war on Turkey. At this stage neither Austria nor Russia wanted to be dragged into war and therefore concluded an agreement at Reichstadt in Bohemia (July 1876).

The Reichstadt agreement established Austro-Hungarian predominance in the western Balkans and Russian predominance in the eastern Balkans. Events soon rendered the agreement obsolete. The Turkish armies defeated the Serbs and the revolt spread to Bulgaria. Turkey then rejected a proposal put forth by all the powers that she should grant autonomy (but not sovereignty) to Bosnia and Bulgaria. Russia thereupon declared war on Turkey, but prior to this she secured the benevolent neutrality of Austria. Austria was in fact too weak militarily, and too isolated diplomatically, to oppose Russia. Nevertheless, she secured agreement at the Budapest Convention (January 1877) that in the event of a Russian victory Austria would receive the right to occupy autonomous Bosnia and Herzegovina, while Russia would confine her military operations to the eastern Balkans. Again, events moved faster than the statesmen. Russia swept through Rumania, single-handedly drove Turkey out of Europe and confronted the Great Powers with the Treaty of San Stefano (March 1878). The terms of the treaty were totally unacceptable to Austria, for they envisaged an enlarged Bulgaria under Russian occupation and thus violated the Reichstadt and Budapest agreements (**130**).

Andrássy persuaded Britain and Germany to revise the Treaty of San Stefano at a general European meeting, the Congress of Berlin (1878). But with the Three Emperors' League in ruins and Bismarck committed to act only as an 'honest broker', the position of Austria-Hungary did not appear very rosy. However, the creation of a 'Big' Bulgaria at San Stefano offended not only the great powers, but also the small, non-Bulgarian peoples in the Balkans and therefore disposed them towards an Austrian solution. The Congress proved to be the crowning success of Andrássy's diplomatic career. Its main achievement was the break-up of Bulgaria into three parts: the northernmost part was left as an autonomous principality; Eastern Rumelia became a semi-autonomous province; and Macedonia was restored to Turkish rule. In addition, Rumania, Serbia and Montenegro achieved independence.

Apart from Bulgaria, the main issue of the Congress was Bosnia and Herzegovina. Austria was anxious lest the two provinces break loose from Turkey and fall into the hands of Serbia and Montenegro and thus upset the delicate balance in the western Balkans. Franz Joseph wanted outright annexation of the provinces as a once-and-for-all solution to the problem of the Empire's southern frontier, but Andrássy counselled caution in view of the domestic hostility to annexation and opposition from Turkey (**9**). He settled for occupation and got it with the approval of the other European powers. Occupation of the two provinces, plus the right to station a garrison in the Sanjak of Novi-Bazar, effectively separated Serbia from Montenegro and provided a gate through which Austria might later expand in the southern Balkans.

From the viewpoint of Great Power rivalry Andrássy could claim to have secured (with the approval of Britain, France and Germany) Austria's economic and strategic interests in the western Balkans against Russia. But as we shall see in chapter 9, the newly occupied territories of Bosnia and Herzegovina proved extraordinarily difficult to accept; by the first decade of the twentieth century they had turned out to be ghosts at the imperial banquet (**21**). In the 1870s very few voices protested against Austria's failure to pay any attention to the growth of Slav nationalism, both inside and outside the Empire. A distinguished exception was Adolf Fischhof, the old revolutionary of 1848, who clearly foresaw the consequences of a foreign policy hatched by diplomats in ignorance of the wishes of the people [**doc. 14**]. Dynastic aggrandisement, albeit for defensive reasons, was uppermost in the minds of the policy-makers of the time.

The final achievement of Andrássy's political career and the logical conclusion to his search for an ally was the Dual Alliance agreed with Germany in 1879. Both Austria and Germany were nervous about Russian intentions after the Congress of Berlin and hence concluded a secret, purely defensive, alliance, which stipulated that if either party were attacked by Russia the other would be obliged to help the party attacked; if either were attacked by another power the other would be obliged to observe benevolent neutrality [**doc. 15**]. The Dual Alliance was renewed regularly until 1918, making it the longest-lasting peacetime alliance of the period. It is difficult to see what advantage Germany derived from the alliance, since Austria was not obliged to support her in the case of a war against France. Austria, by contrast, received precisely the support she needed in the event of an attack by Russia. It became the foundation stone of Austrian foreign policy and the Emperor never questioned it (**17**). The Dual Alliance represented in foreign affairs what the 1867 Compromise had stood for in domestic affairs; the predominance of the Germanic (and Hungarian) elements in the Empire and beyond (**21**).

Austria and the alliance system, 1879–95

Andrássy's policy of containing Russia by a system of alliances was continued by his successors, Baron Haymerle (1879–81) and Count Kálnoky (1881–95). Bismarck, who saw the Dual Alliance as a step towards the re-creation of the Three Emperors' League, induced Austria to join a new Three Emperors' Alliance Treaty in 1881. In addition to a general clause binding the signatories to a benevolent neutrality should any of them become engaged in war with a fourth power, the three signatories renounced the use of force against Turkey. Russia won formal reaffirmation of the principle of closure of the Straits by Turkey to warlike operations, but also agreed that Austria might annex Bosnia and Herzegovina (though not necessarily the Sanjak) when she wished. The treaty certainly left Austria no weaker in the Balkans than she had been before (**130**).

Austria consolidated her position in the next two years by concluding treaties with Serbia, Italy and Rumania. Serbia was the key to Austria's Balkan strategy. Count Kálnoky summed up the Austrian position with disarming frankness in 1881:

> I cannot avoid expressing my well-considered conviction that the pivot of our power position in the south-east lies in Belgrade. As long as we are not firmly established there, whether directly or indirectly, we remain constantly on the defensive on the Danube, the Lim and even on the Sava. If Serbia, by whatever means, is subordinate to our influence, or better still, if we are the masters in Serbia, then we can be at ease concerning our possession of Bosnia and its appendages and our position on the lower Danube and in Rumania. Only then will our power in the Balkans rest on a firm basis which accords with the important interests of the monarchy (**148**).

For the time being Kálnoky was content to have 'a peaceful and flourishing independent Serbia in friendly relations with us' (**15**). King Milan obliged in 1881 by agreeing to railway links with the Monarchy and a commercial treaty, valid for ten years, which admitted Serbian agricultural exports into Austria–Hungary on favourable terms. This was followed by a secret political treaty in which Serbia agreed not to conclude any treaties with a foreign power without Austria's permission; to renounce any designs on the occupied provinces and the Sanjak; and finally to tolerate no agitation against the Monarchy on Serbian soil, including Bosnia and Herzegovina. In return, Austria agreed to support Serbia's claim to Macedonia in the event of the collapse of Turkish rule. These treaties turned Serbia into a satellite state of Austria, economically and politically. Unfortunately for Austria, they were the handiwork of King Milan and had little support among the Serbian population (**132**).

In 1882 Italy became Austria's ally by signing the Triple Alliance, which upheld the monarchic principle and committed Austria–Hungary to help Italy only in the unlikely event of an unprovoked attack by France. Austria had no illusions about the value of Italy as an ally, but was content to secure her neutrality in the event of a possible war in the east. If anti-French feeling drew Italy towards Austria, it was anti-Russian feeling which prompted Rumania to sign a treaty alliance with Austria in 1883. Rumania resented Russian treatment of her after 1878 and even feared for her independence. Although over three million Rumanians lived, disenfranchised, within the Hungarian half of the Empire, Rumania concluded a secret, defensive treaty with the Empire, which provided the latter with valuable military cover in the south-east against a possible Russian attack (**137**).

The Three Emperors' Alliance was irrevocably split by the Bulgarian crisis of 1885–86. By a bizarre turn of events Austria and Russia suddenly found their roles reversed over Bulgaria. In 1885 a nationalist coup in Eastern Rumelia led to its union with the Principality of Bulgaria. Russia was opposed to it, Austria wavered, Bulgaria went to war with Serbia and won, and finally the ruler, Prince Alexander, was kidnapped by Russian officers. Bulgaria then elected a prince of the House of Coburg, who was supported by Austria but opposed by Russia. The crisis passed and Bulgaria asserted her independence; but the Three Emperors' Alliance was not renewed in 1887 and Austria and Russia were never again allies (**130**).

Kálnoky's chief foreign-policy aim during his fourteen years in office (1881–95) was to prevent the monarchy from being encircled in the south by a ring of Russian satellite states (**135**). The Three Emperors' Alliance was the first casualty of the Bulgarian crisis, but this loss was offset by the Mediterranean Agreement concluded between Austria, Britain and Italy in 1887. This was designed to uphold the *status quo* in the Mediterranean and safeguard Sofia, Constantinople and the Straits from Russian interference; it served Austria's interests well.

Russia may have been successfully excluded from south-eastern Europe during these years, but Austria's own Balkan alliances were not in a healthy state. The alliance with Serbia was a link with the dynasty and lacked roots in the people. When the unstable King Milan abdicated in 1889 the dynasty was only saved at the last moment by a regency for his 13-year-old son, Alexander, who kept on the Austrian connection. Austria's alliance with Rumania was also a treaty concluded with the king without the knowledge or approval of the population as a whole. Relations between the two countries were strained by a tariff war in the late 1880s, as well as by a strong irredentist movement in Rumania, which fed on the Hungarian maltreatment of Rumanians in Transylvania. Austria's relations with Italy were also marred by a powerful irredentist movement in the latter. Roughly 3.25 million Rumanians and 750,000 Italians lived inside the Habsburg Monarchy before World War One. Both Rumania and Italy, therefore, persistently demanded the return of their 'unredeemed' (*irredenta*) lands and this agitation cut across the foreign-policy interests of the Monarchy. The Triple Alliance itself, in spite of periodic renewals, was unpopular with Italian public opinion and was only adhered to out of fear of France (**130**).

Austro-Russian co-operation, 1895–1906

By the mid-1890s it had become apparent that Austria's defensive alliance system was in decline. Russia, however, was not wholly antagonistic to Austria at this time, partly because she was turning her attention to the Far East. Kálnoky's successor, Goluchowski (1895–1906), failed to renew the Mediterranean Agreement with Britain and turned instead to Russia (**134**). He concluded an *entente* in 1897 to preserve the *status quo*, observe the principle of non-interference and renounce all designs of conquest in the Balkan states. Goluchowski told the Austrian council of ministers that 'we can avoid conflict with Russia without giving up any of our vital interests' (**130**). This important agreement, which lasted ten years, was viewed by many Austrians, including the future foreign minister Aehrenthal, as the first step towards a more far-reaching understanding with Russia. It was not to be so because of events which took place after 1900 both inside and outside the Monarchy.

The first test of the Austro-Russian *entente* came in 1903, when open rebellion broke out among the South Slavs in Macedonia, strategically the most important province of the Ottoman Empire in Europe. Austria and Russia wished to preserve the *status quo* in the area and signed the Mürzsteg Programme (1903), which confirmed their 1897 agreement and established an international gendarmerie to keep order and supervise reforms in the province.

Austria's policy in the Balkans remained unchanged in the years after 1903. Russia was preoccupied with the Far East at this time, suffering military defeat at the hands of Japan and undergoing a domestic revolution in 1904–5. But Austria, owing to her domestic problems and weak military position, was unable to reassert her influence in the Balkans (**148**). The Mürzsteg Programme remained in force and the years 1903–06 have been called 'the high-water mark of the Austro-Russian entente' (**130**). Yet by 1907 Europe was virtually divided into two power blocs, the Triple Alliance and the Triple Entente. Goluchowski's foreign policy was based on maintaining good relations with Germany and Italy. But the Moroccan crisis of 1905, which was essentially a diplomatic trial of strength between Germany and France, revealed just how isolated the two

Germanic Central Powers were and called into question the policy of the *status quo* in the Balkans. Goluchowksi was forced to resign in 1906.

8   The Drift to War: 1906–14

The crucial decisions which settled the fate of the Habsburg Monarchy were made in the decade before the outbreak of World War One in 1914. The nationality disputes between Czechs and Germans within Austria, and between Austrians and Hungarians within the Dual Monarchy, were never solved, but at least they remained internal problems. After 1900 the growth of the South Slav movement made the nationality problem a foreign-policy question, which was only resolved by war in 1914 (**148**).

In the early years of the twentieth century the internal weakness of Austria–Hungary was gradually overshadowed by her vulnerability in foreign affairs. The relative stability of the Balkans in the 1880s and 1890s gave way to turbulence and uncertainty as a result of three interrelated events: the collapse of Turkey; the resurgence of Russian interest in the Balkans; and the rising strength of South Slav nationalism. The collapse of Turkey brought Russia and Austria face to face in the Balkans for the first time. But the immediate danger to the Habsburg Empire, within and without, came from South Slav nationalism [**doc. 17**] (**141**). The Austrian government could never decide whether to use force against the South Slavs, or to placate them by concessions. A policy of masterly inactivity was pursued. The result, in A.F. Pribram's words, was that 'the South Slav sore, allowed to fester on the body of the Empire, spread over it until it brought about its death' (**138**).

Aehrenthal and the policy of expansion, 1906–12

There was no shortage of panaceas put forth by Austrian statesmen to reverse the monarchy's deteriorating position in the Balkans. Aehrenthal (foreign minister, 1906–12) sought by active diplomacy to reassert Habsburg power and influence in the western Balkans; Conrad von Hötzendorf (army chief of staff, 1906–11; 1912–17) argued for a preventive war against Serbia and Italy; Franz Ferdinand (nephew of Franz Joseph and heir to the throne) hoped to reduce Hungary to the status of a Habsburg Crownland, create a centralised state and then crush the South Slav revolution (**131**, **143**, **146**). All these plans foundered on one obstacle – the Emperor. He had the last word in foreign policy and his policy was one of peace, almost at any price. Once, when Hötzendorf attacked Aehrenthal, Franz Joseph intervened and reproved the General personally:

> I forbid you these continuous attacks against Aehrenthal. These attacks because of the Balkan policy and of Italy, they are directed against me, for I make this policy, it is my policy. My policy is that of peace. To this policy all must adjust themselves (**17**).

The experience of his long reign had taught Franz Joseph that war always brought disaster to the Empire. Austria had lost Italy in a war against France in 1859 and she had lost the German Empire in a war against Prussia in 1866. Might she not lose her Balkan possessions in a war against Russia? Given these considerations it is hardly surprising that Franz Joseph strove for 60 years 'more single-mindedly than any other individual to keep the peace of Europe' (**4**).

The fact remains that Austria's policy of peace became increasingly incompatible with her status as a Great Power. The crunch came with the assassination of Franz Ferdinand at Sarajevo. The mere desire for peace among statesmen does not always avert war. The historian needs to look beyond the motives of the actors and ask whether the policies they implemented had the effect of bringing war closer. In the case of Austria–Hungary the important question would seem to be not whether Franz Joseph sought peace, but why he retained so much political power and what consequences this had on foreign policy. There is conflicting opinion about whether Austria's foreign policy was essentially aggressive or defensive in the decade before 1914. Some historians have seen her foreign policy as a desperate attempt to solve the intractable domestic problems which plagued the Monarchy in the pre-war years (**21, 132, 136**). Others have depicted her foreign policy as moderate to a fault in the face of a ring of provocative Balkan states backed by the imperial might of Tsarist Russia (**17, 138**).

Goluchowski's policy of maintaining the *status quo* had been subjected to increasing criticism in Vienna before he resigned in 1906. The alternative was to seek closer links with Russia in the hope of eventually reviving the Three Emperors' Alliance; in short, to recreate the security of the 1880s. The problem was how to achieve this aim while at the same time increasing Austria's influence in the Balkans. The man appointed to resolve this problem was Baron von

Aehrenthal, Austrian foreign minister from 1906 to 1912 and the most energetic and controversial occupant of the post since Metternich (**150**). Both the aims and methods of Aehrenthal's diplomacy aroused strong emotions: King Edward VII called him a 'slippery man'; Joseph Redlich called him 'the last great old Austrian' (**17**). It is ironic that Aehrenthal, a former ambassador at St Petersburg and the man who sought a rapprochement with Russia, should have gone down in history as the man who permanently ruined relations with Russia.

Aehrenthal's overriding aim was to revive the prestige of the Monarchy by reasserting its supremacy in the western half of the Balkans [**doc. 16**]. He believed that this could be done only if Austria–Hungary became less dependent on her ally, Germany, and improved relations with her potential enemies (**146**). He had little success with Russia, whose foreign minister, Izvolsky, was under the influence of liberal opinion at home and sought closer relations with Britain and France in order to further Russia interests in the Near East. Although the days of the Austro-Russian *entente* were obviously numbered, Aehrenthal chose this time to put forth his plans for a railway link in the Sanjak of Novi-Bazar. The Sanjak railway would join up with the Bosnian line and provide a direct link with Turkey and make Serbia even more dependent on the Monarchy (**147**).

Austria had the legal right to build a railway in the Sanjak under the Berlin Treaty but Aehrenthal misjudged the Russian reaction. In her wrath Russia persuaded Britain not to cooperate with Austria–Hungary any longer in Macedonia, thus ending the Mürzsteg Agreement. But the Austro-Russian *entente* was not yet finished. Indeed, Izvolsky himself proposed that if Austria promised to support Russia's claim for the free passage of warships through the Straits, then Russia would not object to the Habsburgs annexing Bosnia, Herzegovina and the Sanjak.

Bosnia and Herzegovina had been occupied by Austria–Hungary since 1878, but they were still under Turkish sovereignty. Negotiations between Austria and Russia had already begun when the Young Turk revolution broke out in 1908 and brought a revival of Turkish nationalism and the threat, from the Austrian viewpoint, of a reaffirmation of Turkish influence over the two provinces. Aehrenthal therefore decided on a speedy annexation (**139**). His motives for annexation, the negotiations, and the consequences of the annexation, have aroused fierce controversy among historians (**9**, **17**, **21**, **136**). What is not in doubt is the fact that the Bosnian crisis of 1908 marked a turning point in both Austro-Hungarian foreign policy and in relations among the great powers in the Balkans.

What were Aehrenthal's motives? Was the annexation planned as the first step towards the incorporation of Serbia into the Habsburg dominions? There is some evidence for the view that Aehrenthal anticipated the collapse of Turkey and hoped to secure Austria's influence in the Balkans through the creation of a South Slav group (including Serbia, Bosnia–Herzegovina and Croatia–Slavonia) within the Empire (**146**). On the other hand, the annexation of Bosnia–Herzegovina has been interpreted by F.R.Bridge as 'a conservative move' by Austria–Hungary designed to end the ambiguous position of the two provinces and pave the way for reform, as well as drawing a clear line between Austro-Hungarian and Turkish frontiers (**130**). According to this interpretation, the annexation of Bosnia–Herzegovina was undertaken as compensation for Austria's renunciation of her rights over the Sanjak (**25**).

The negotiations between Austria and Russia leading up to the annexation took place at Berchtold's castle in Buchlau, Moravia, in September 1908. What actually passed between the vain Izvolsky and the ambitious Aehrenthal at Buchlau has never been established, because no agreed written record was kept of their conversations (**139**). Therein lay the problem. It seems, however, that Russia agreed in principle to Austria's annexation of Bosnia and Herzegovina in return for a sympathetic Austrian attitude towards Russia's desire for a free passage through the Straits. Austria and Russia also agreed to put these questions before a conference, but it was left unclear whether the conference was to authorise the annexation or merely ratify it. Izvolsky then left for a leisurely tour of the capitals of western Europe. One month later Franz Joseph proclaimed the annexation of the two provinces without consulting the Russians. On the next day Bulgaria declared her independence.

The annexation of Bosnia and Herzegovina hit Europe like a bombshell and began a six-month diplomatic crisis which almost led to a general war (**142**). The Austro-Russian *entente* was now irrevocably destroyed. But most serious of all, the annexation unleashed a wave of Slav nationalism which ultimately engulfed all the Great Powers in the Balkans (**132**).

As a result of Aehrenthal's precipitate action in 1908 Russia was convinced that the annexation of Bosnia was the first step in an Austrian plan to march on Salonika. But in fact Aehrenthal had little choice after the annexation to pursue any policy other than that of maintaining the *status quo*. In spite of his personal dynamism, it is mistaken to see Aehrenthal as an expansionist; he was closer to an

Austrian Bismarck, who had limited aims and always hoped to keep the diplomatic lines open to St. Petersburg (**130**). In three areas under Turkish control of influence – Crete, Albania and Macedonia – Aehrenthal refused to interfere and thereby convinced the Great Powers of the sincerity of his adherence to the *status quo*. The Monarchy's main fear was that Russia would organise a Balkan league against her. This fear did not materialise in 1909 and 1910 because Serbia, Bulgaria and Greece could not agree on how to partition Macedonia, while at the same time Serbia and Montenegro were locked in a dynastic quarrel (**15**).

The Monarchy's relations with Italy deteriorated after the annexation. In 1909 Italy joined with Russia under the Racconigi Agreement to maintain the *status quo* in the Balkans. Italy was seen by many Austrians as the real enemy, despite her membership of the Triple Alliance. Conrad von Hötzendorf, the Austrian Chief of Staff, repeatedly called for a preventive war against Italy, and Archduke Franz Ferdinand in his military capacity devoted much time to preparing for such an eventuality (**133**). Aehrenthal took a different view and improved relations with Italy by remaining neutral in the Italo-Turkish War of 1912. Aehrenthal had won the ear of Franz Joseph and the latter curtly dismissed Hötzendorf in 1911 for opposing a policy of peace (**17**).

Berchtold and the Balkan crises, 1912–13

Aehrenthal's death in February 1912 brought no sudden change in Austrian foreign policy. Count Berchtold, his successor, was a wealthy aristocrat who came out of retirement from a sense of duty, not ambition. Unlike Aehrenthal, he had no ideas for the reconstruction of the Monarchy, but was a conventional – or, many would say, complacent – supporter of the dualist system. Perhaps Berchtold's most positive idea was his belief in the diplomacy of the Concert of Europe as the best way to solve international disputes (**130**). He came to office just after the Moroccan crisis and Libyan War had shaken the Turkish Empire and sparked off a series of crises in the Balkans which presented the Monarchy with its greatest challenge (**149**).

In the summer of 1912 a major political and military crisis gripped Turkey and provoked the Balkan states to drive the Turks out of Europe. Berchtold tried, without success, to forestall any action by the Balkan states by an appeal to the Concert of Europe. In October 1912 a Balkan League, composed of Bulgaria, Serbia, Greece and

Montenegro, drove Turkey out of Europe to within 48 kilometres of Constantinople. Joseph Redlich wrote in his diary on 28 October: 'The sick man is dead. Austria has every chance to be the sick man in his place' (**29**). Berchtold accepted the new situation with one proviso: Serbia must not be allowed to extend her frontiers to the Adriatic because it was feared that a Serbian port would one day become a Russian port (**130**). Berchtold's announcement sparked off a crisis in Austro-Serbian relations which was made worse by Russia's support for Serbia. But at this point the Triple Alliance pulled together and stood firm on the question of a Serbian port and Russia withdrew her support for her ally. The question was finally settled at the London Conference (May 1913), where the great powers accepted Berchtold's idea of an independent Albania. But the settlement still left Serbia and Montenegro substantially enlarged, sharing borders with Austria–Hungary and eager for revenge. As Pašić, the Serbian prime minister, said: 'The first round is over, now we must prepare for the second against Austria' (**15**).

Thwarted in her desire for an Adriatic port, Serbia, joined by Greece, claimed areas of Macedonia which had been awarded to Bulgaria after the first Balkan War. Berchtold took the opportunity to support Bulgaria in an attempt to cut the arch enemy, Serbia, down to size. But his plan foundered on Rumania, who refused to stay neutral (she claimed territory from Bulgaria and had long-standing irredentist claims against Hungary). In the second Balkan War in 1913 Serbia, Greece and Rumania crushed Bulgaria. Serbia gained most of northern Macedonia by the Treaty of Bucharest (August 1913) (**130**).

Berchtold's foreign policy had relied first on the Concert of Europe, and second on Bulgaria, to keep the *status quo* in the Balkans and to contain Serbia (**138**). That policy was now in ruins: Austria was face to face with the problem of Serbia and, at one remove, Russia (**25**). Joseph Redlich's diary entry for 30 October 1913 reads:

> The situation for Austria in the Balkans is very serious. Either we follow events and let Greater-Serbia build itself: then we lose Bosnia and perhaps Croatia as soon as Russia arms and begins war. Or we dictate a customs union with Serbia which they refuse and lead us into war. I don't see anything good from this war (**29**).

Austria–Hungary now had limited room for manoeuvre and frequently found herself at odds with her own allies. Germany's Balkan policy revolved around Greece, while Austria hoped to bring Bulgaria into the Triple Alliance. Rumania nursed grievances against both Bulgaria and the Magyars and was always on the verge of leaving the Triple Alliance. Finally, Italy clashed with Austria over Albania and Trieste and left her ally in no doubt that she would not fulfil any of her alliance commitments (**138**).

Serbia not only harboured terrorist groups which operated within the Monarchy, but she was working towards the formation of a new Balkan league which, according to the Vienna newspaper, the *Neue Freie Presse*, would be 'a dagger in the hand of Russia pointed straight at the heart of Austria' (**130**). Berchtold hoped to arrest Austria's deteriorating position by a diplomatic offensive. A Foreign Ministry official drew up a memorandum calling for Germany to join Austria–Hungary in blocking any attempt by the Triple Entente powers to complete the encirclement of the Monarchy from the south. The memorandum contained not a hint of war. Nor did it become the basis of policy: four days after it was written Archduke Franz Ferdinand and his wife were assassinated in Sarajevo on 28 June 1914 (**130**).

Sarajevo and the outbreak of war

Five weeks passed between the assassination at Sarajevo and the outbreak of war. It cannot be accepted as a foregone conclusion that war against Serbia would be the next step for Austria to take (**133**). In Vienna, at the popular level at least, the mood was not at all warlike. Franz Ferdinand had never been popular with the people and a few days after the crime Joseph Redlich noted the widespread apathy in the city: 'No one wants to know about serious measures against Serbia from where the crime was doubtless organized' (**29**). But at the Ballhausplatz some action had to be decided upon. Berchtold was caught in a difficult position. On the one hand, Conrad von Hötzendorf saw in the Sarajevo murder a heaven-sent opportunity to launch a preventive war against Serbia; on the other hand, Franz Joseph and Count Tisza, the Hungarian prime minister, were opposed to war against Serbia (**144**). Berchtold knew that failure to take vigorous action would be regarded as a clear 'renunciation of our Great Power position' (**9, 130**).

It has frequently been argued that Austria–Hungary chose to go to war against Serbia in 1914 because she had failed to solve her internal problems (**21, 136, 143**). There is something to be said for this argument, which will be examined in the next chapter on war guilt. But it must be remembered that in 1914 the threat facing

Austria was a foreign one (**130**). The Monarchy was burdened with many unsolved national problems, but it would be false to imagine that in 1914 it was on the verge of collapse.

From the military viewpoint the situation was not favourable to Austria (**143**). Her standing army had been recently increased to just under half a million. But Russia had planned in 1913 to increase the size of her army by that amount alone to a wartime strength of two million within five years. Time was on the side of Russia. Austria's diplomatic position was not much stronger. It seemed unlikely that either Italy or Rumania would support Austria. The Monarchy's one dependable ally was Germany, and her action in the July crisis provides the key to understanding Austria's own behaviour (**133**). Germany had reasons of her own for urging Austria to take a strong line against Serbia. She feared that a failure to act on Austria's part would result in a new Balkan league directed from St. Petersburg, which would cut off Austria and Germany from the Near East.

Germany took the fateful decision to support Austria on 5 July. Emboldened by Germany's support, Berchtold successfully persuaded Tisza of the need to take a firm stand (**144**). The Ballhausplatz then proceeded in a rather leisurely fashion to draft an ultimatum to Serbia which, if accepted, would have reduced the latter to a satellite of the Monarchy (**132**). The note was presented to Serbia on 23 July. Berchtold's major worry at this stage was that Serbia might actually accept it. His wife said later that 'poor Leopold could not sleep on the day when he wrote his ultimatum to the Serbs as he was so worried that they might accept it. Several times during the night he got up and altered or added some clause, to reduce this risk' (**15**).

Berchtold's fears proved unjustified. Serbia rejected the note and Austria declared war on 28 July; Russia mobilised on 30 July; Germany declared war on Russia on 1 August and on France on 3 August. The general European war had begun.

The question why the murder of the heir to the Habsburg throne by one of his own teenage subjects, Gavrilo Princip, in a rebellious province, Bosnia, led to a general European war cannot be adequately answered by looking at the affairs of Austria–Hungary alone. The Great Powers had got themselves locked into two competing alliance systems which left them little room for manoeuvre. The two powers most immediately concerned with events in the Balkans – Russia and Germany – felt that they had to stand fast in 1914: Russia in support of Serbia and Germany in support of

Austria–Hungary. Austria was intent on punishing Serbia for the crime at Sarajevo and mistakenly thought that a war against her southern neighbour could be localised.

The cry of 'gallant little Serbia' which sprang up in Britain after the start of the war was absent before July 1914 (**4**). Indeed, it is fair to say that in the decade before 1914 the European powers frequently expected Austria to take military action against Serbia. Serbia had been subjected to centuries of oppressive Turkish rule and retained some of the habits of conspiratorial violence when the tyranny suddenly ended (**141**). Dimitrijević, the Serbian chief of intelligence, was the dominating force behind the Black Hand, the secret society which masterminded the assassination of Franz Ferdinand (**131**). Pašić, the prime minister, was probably sincere in his attempts to reach an accommodation with Austria but he was unable to expose the activities of the Black Hand for fear of appearing too pro-Austrian (**25**). In an age when the doctrine of national self-determination was not universally accepted as the basis of a country's frontiers, the pan-Slav activities of Serbia did not meet with approval everywhere. With the exception of Russia, most countries regarded Serbia as a nuisance (**4**, **5**). The British ambassador in Vienna compared the trouble which Serbia caused Austria to the hostile attitude which the Transvaal Republic had taken towards Great Britain a few year earlier (**130**).

The question frequently asked in Austria–Hungary at this time was not why she took action against Serbia in 1914, but why she had not done so earlier. It is estimated that the Chief of Staff, Conrad von Hötzendorf, had urged war against Serbia no fewer than 25 times in the years 1913–14 (**132**). As we have seen, the advice was firmly rejected by the Emperor himself. It is the view of many Austrian historians (e.g., Redlich, Pribram, Hantsch) that Habsburg foreign policy, with the possible exception of the annexation of Bosnia–Herzegovina, was essentially a defensive policy designed to keep the peace. It is certainly true that Austria wished to avoid upsetting the delicate balance of power in the Balkans. To this extent her policy was a peaceful, defensive one. But at the same time she had no positive strategy for dealing with the problem of South Slav nationalism (**148**).

The negative face of Habsburg foreign policy was revealed after events in the Balkans in 1912–13 had changed the situation dramatically (**138**). Turkey was driven from Europe and the problem of South Slav irredentism in the form of an enlarged Serbia suddenly became a threat to the very existence of Austria–Hungary. The threat

lay in the combination of irredentism backed for the first time by a
major power, Russia (**130**). In the late nineteenth century Russia
was too weak to threaten Austria's vital interests in the Balkans. In
the early years of the twentieth century she was too preoccupied in
the Far East. But after 1905 Russia again turned her attention to the
Balkans. Austria's policy of inaction had proved to be a wasting
asset. By June 1914 it was widely recognised in Vienna that some
form of drastic action was necessary to save the Monarchy's status
as a Great Power.

9 'War Guilt' and the South Slav Question

Foreign policy has to do with diplomacy and it was diplomacy which unleashed the war. Therefore the question of responsibility for causing the war – the so-called 'war guilt' question – which has occupied historians for so long, has centred on diplomatic investigations. But the trouble with this approach is that it asks only a limited range of questions. The emphasis is placed on diplomatic events and questions are rarely asked about more deep-seated attitudes and institutions which may have determined certain courses of action.

We have seen in chapter 8 that a plausible case can be made for the view that Austria's foreign policy in the Balkans was essentially defensive. But was this enough to avert war? How vigorously did the Monarchy seek an alternative to war? How many problems, both domestic and foreign, were left unsolved, thus increasing the likelihood of war?

The basic problem confronting the Habsburg Empire in the decade before 1914 was the movement towards South Slav unity (**19**). It was both an internal and an external problem because the frontiers of the Empire cut right through the body of South Slavs: twice as many South Slavs (7,300,000) lived inside the Monarchy as outside it (3,300,000) [**doc. 17**]. In an age of nationalism it was extremely unlikely that the union of all South Slavs could be prevented. The question was whether it would occur inside or outside the Empire. In a letter to Franz Ferdinand, dated 14 December 1914, Conrad von Hötzendorf put the choice facing the monarchy:

> The unification of the South Slav race is one of the powerful national movements which can neither be ignored nor kept down. The question can only be, whether unification will take place within the boundaries of the Monarchy – that is at the expense of Serbia's independence – or under Serbia's leadership at the expense of the Monarchy. The cost to the Monarchy would be the loss of its South Slav provinces and thus of almost its entire coastline. The loss of territory and prestige would relegate the Monarchy to the status of a small power (**133**).

The South Slav problem can best be studied by examining two separate, but interrelated aspects of it: (1) the relationship between the Habsburg Monarchy and Serbia; (2) the Austro–Hungarian administration of Bosnia–Herzegovina.

The Habsburg Monarchy and Serbia

The first aspect of the South Slav problem concerns the Monarchy's relations with Serbia. Serbia, like Croatia, had a long history; in 1389 she had been defeated by the Turks at the battle of Kossovo. Strangely, it was the memory of Kossovo which held the Serb people together during centuries of Turkish rule (**4**). When she achieved independence in 1878 Serbia was recognised by all the Great Powers as being within the Habsburg sphere of influence, both economically and diplomatically. Until 1903 the pro-Austrian, Obrenović dynasty ruled Serbia, but it failed to keep in touch with the people and was toppled in that year by a group of nationalist conspirators who offered the throne to a member of the rival dynasty, Peter Karageorgević (**59**). Behind the Serbian throne stood the powerful Radical Party, which campaigned for the unification of all Serbs under the new dynasty. Nationalist societies sprang up and extended their activities into Macedonia, Bosnia–Herzegovina and Croatia–Slovenia (**31**). Serbia had now become the 'cradle' of the Serb national movement and the Piedmont of all the South Slavs (**30**).

It was mainly the actions of Austria–Hungary which forced Serbia into an independent economic and political path. Most important was the so-called 'pig war' (1906), which probably did more than anything else to turn Serbia into an irreconcilable enemy of the Empire (**10**). The latter had traditionally taken over 80 per cent of Serbia's exports (mainly livestock), but when Serbia placed a large munitions order with a French firm, instead of with Skoda in Bohemia, Austria retaliated by closing the frontier to Serbian livestock. The big landed interests in Austria and Hungary obviously benefited from the exclusion of Serbian produce, but the effect of the pig war in Serbia was to end her commercial dependence on the Monarchy and instil in the people a lasting hatred of the Habsburgs (**132**).

The annexation of Bosnia–Herzegovina (1908) was a severe blow to Serbia, but it would be wrong to assume that a reconciliation between Serbia and Austria–Hungary was impossible, even in the years following it. The diaries of J.M. Baernreither, a member of the

Austrian Delegations and a leading expert on the South Slav question, show unmistakably that Serbia could have been reconciled to Austria if the latter had liberalised trade and communications between the two countries and reached some agreement over Macedonia [**doc. 18**] (**25**). But these suggestions were rebuffed by Aehrenthal, whose only policy seemed to be the negative one of blocking Serbia's access to the sea. The Monarchy's failure to conciliate Serbia was rooted in its internal contradictions, in particular the entrenched supremacy enjoyed by the Magyar and German-speaking groups (**19, 148**). This point was well put during the war years by the Chief of the Cabinet of Emperor Charles, Count Polzer Hoditz:

> Nobody thought of revising our Balkan policy, for this would have involved a complete change also in the inner policy. The understanding that the hatred of Serbia and Rumania ... was caused by ourselves, by our customs policy, that the Southern Slavs did not want anything else than to unite themselves and to get an outlet to the sea, that by our unfortunate Albanian policy we have closed the last valve and therefore an explosion became inevitable: this understanding was never attained by the ruling elements (**10**).

The Austro–Hungarian administration of Bosnia–Herzegovina

The second aspect of the South Slav problem concerns the joint Austro–Hungarian administration of Bosnia–Herzegovina. The decision taken at the Congress of Berlin (1878) authorising Austria–Hungary to occupy Bosnia–Herzegovina has been described by the Yugoslav historian, Vladimir Dedijer, as a 'fatal' one because the inclusion of 1,200,000 South Slavs upset the already precarious balance of nationalities within the Empire (**132**). But this is to pre-judge the issue, for as with the other aspects of the South Slav problem, so much depended on how Austria–Hungary handled it. Under the autocratic administration of Benjamin Kállay (1882–1903) Bosnia–Herzegovina enjoyed security, an end to corruption and the beginnings of an extensive modernisation programme (**57**). Unfortunately, all this was accompanied by a 90 per cent illiteracy rate, divide-and-rule tactics, and the retention of a feudal system of landholding which left half the population in the villages, the Christian *kmets*, in a position of serfdom (**15**).

It is not easy to judge, even in hindsight, what constitutes a successful administration of a territory. A contemporary defender of

Austria's record in Bosnia–Herzegovina, Heinrich Lammasch, likened Kállay's administration to Lord Cromer's in Egypt and called them both 'the best types of colonial governments' [**doc. 19**]. This may have been the case, but it did not prevent the growth of discontent in the two provinces. Almost half of the population were Orthodox Serbs and a majority of them probably wanted union with Serbia. The Moslems (30 per cent) in the provinces preferred Austrian rule, while the Roman Catholic Croats (25 per cent) were perhaps divided in their allegiances to Austria and Serbia (**4**). What proved crucial in the end, however, was not the views of the majority, but the actions of a fanatical minority.

Out of the primitive villages in Bosnia at the turn of the century a generation of young romantic rebels rose in revolt against Habsburg rule. Austria's policy of suppressing all political activity and holding back on educational reforms doubtless aggravated the situation in Bosnia. It is an open question whether Austria could have drawn the revolutionary sting from the Young Bosnian Movement if she had taken a more liberal policy towards the province. In the event the crime committed by one young Bosnian in Sarajevo was hatched in a secret society, the Black Hand, which had been nourished on the idea of tyrannicide; it reflected the backward society from which it came. In the words of one historian it was 'the most amateurish political homicide in modern history' (**131**).

Dualism and the South Slav problem

The solution to both aspects of the South Slav problem ultimately foundered on the dualist constitution. Any move towards unification of South Slavs within the Empire would have meant an end to dualism and the breakdown of German–Magyar hegemony (**12, 148**). The one man who saw the problem clearly was the heir to the throne, Franz Ferdinand. His vision of the future of the Habsburg Monarchy may be seen as a symptom of the disease afflicting it and a measure of the tragic impasse into which it had landed.

Although his actual power was limited, Franz Ferdinand was devoted to a peaceful foreign policy before 1914 (**149**). He also saw beyond diplomacy and spent much time devising plans for a reorganisation of the Empire when he came to the throne. The idea most closely associated with the archduke was trialism, a scheme whereby the Slavs inside and outside the Empire would be brought into a third federative unit, alongside the Germans and Magyars. Yet in spite of this scheme, Franz Ferdinand cannot be seen as a potential saviour of the Monarchy. Recent research has shown that trialism was only part of a tactical move to frighten the Magyars (**131, 132**). He saw the 'preponderance of the Magyars' as the source of all the Monarchy's troubles and he sought to crush them. But he had no intention of granting self-determination to the Slavs (**21**). On the contrary, he envisaged a strong centralised state, buttressed by the Crown and the Army and with the leadership firmly in the hands of the Austro-German elite.

10 World War One and the Collapse of the Empire

Austria–Hungary went to war in August 1914 to solve the South Slav problem once and for all. Four years later, in October 1918, the Empire was defeated and it collapsed. Its final disintegration has an air of inevitability about it when viewed in retrospect. But a close examination of the fateful years 1914–18 shows that the dissolution of the monarchy was not anticipated even by the opponents of the regime, at home and abroad, until the last year of the war. Before this time alternative outcomes were possible, if not probable: victory on the battlefield; a separate peace with the Entente powers; internal reform of the Empire. To understand why these alternatives failed we need to look at the military events of 1914–18 with minds unclouded by notions of historical inevitability.

The Austro-Hungarian army and the war

In Austria–Hungary, as in all other countries in 1914, there was great initial enthusiasm for the war and all the nationalities showed themselves loyal to the Monarchy. The alliance with Germany, dating from 1879, was the constant for Austria in the war years and ultimately the deciding factor in her very existence (**21**). The two Central Powers were joined by Turkey in October 1914, and by Bulgaria in September 1915, to form the so-called Quadruple Alliance, which occupied a continuous stretch of territory from the North Sea to the Anatolian peninsula. Italy took a different path. Although a member of the Triple Alliance, Italy declared her neutrality in August 1914 on the grounds that she had not been notified in time about the Austrian ultimatum to Serbia. Austria's main diplomatic task in the following months was to prevent Italy from joining the Entente powers. Berchtold was willing to cede the Trentino and parts of the Albanian coastline, but Italy's appetite for land grew with the asking and she finally joined the Entente side (Treaty of London, April 1915) in return for the Trentino, Trieste, the most important Dalmatian islands and the southern part of Dalmatia. It is doubtful if Austria could have kept Italy neutral by making more concessions (**162**). As it was, Italy declared war on Austria in May 1915 and became the only power committed to the break-up of the Empire at this early date. Partly for this reason the war against Italy was popular with all the peoples of the Monarchy (**12**).

The instrument charged with carrying out the Empire's foreign policy – the Austro–Hungarian army – was not equal to the task. The problems began long before 1914. The army was actually smaller in proportion to the population in 1914 than it had been in 1870, and much less had been spent on it by Austria than was the case with the armies of any of the other Great Powers. Only one-fifth of those eligible for military service were conscripted, with the result that Austria–Hungary could field only 48 infantry divisions compared to 93 for Russia and 88 for France. The Dual Monarchy was also inferior in firepower. She had fewer pieces of artillery than the other powers and in 1914 was producing only 1 million shells per month, compared to 7 million for Germany and 4 million for Russia (**161**).

The main dilemma for the Habsburg Monarchy was that she had to fight a two-front war with inadequate means. The problem was compounded by the Austrian General Staff, which could not decide before 1914 which of the two fronts – Galicia (against Russia) or Serbia – to treat as more important. The plan of Conrad von Hötzendorf, the Chief of Staff, was to crush Serbia first in a swift offensive and then turn against Russia. But he was unable to shift a major army grouping (B Staffel – 12 divisions) quickly enough from Serbia to Galicia, with the result that Austria suffered a series of disasters in the early months of the war (**145**). Not only had the Austrians been thrown out of Serbia by December 1914, but they were also driven out of eastern Galicia and the Bukovina by the numerically superior Russian forces (**159**).

These early defeats had a devastating effect on the Habsburg army. In the first half-year of fighting three-quarters of a million men were lost, including a high percentage of trained officers. 120,000 men were taken in a single day when the great fortress of Pzemysl fell to the Russians in May 1915 (**15**). But surprisingly the army recovered and by 1916 it had become 'a more formidable instrument than it had been at the outbreak of the war' (**157**).

Austria began to recover from her early disasters, but only with German help and in a way which revealed a dangerous dependence on her stronger partner. In the spring of 1915 the combined Austrian-German forces drove Russia out of Galicia and conquered most of Poland. By the end of the year Austria had taken all of

Serbia and Montenegro, but only with German and Bulgarian help. On the third front of the war the Austrian armies held the numerically superior Italians in eleven battles along the Isonzo River from May 1915 to September 1917. Italy was finally routed at Caporetto in late 1917, with a loss of 600,000 men, but again this was achieved only with the help of Germany (**12, 150**).

Austria's victories exhausted her as much as her defeats and placed her increasingly under the Prussian heel. The turning point came with the Brusilov offensive by Russia in the summer of 1916, when almost the whole eastern front was put under German supreme command. Rumania, encouraged by the Russian victories under Brusilov, entered the war on the Entente side, but was soon eliminated (December 1916) by a joint Austrian-German counteroffensive. By late 1916 the Austrian and German armies controlled a considerable extent of foreign territory and seemed to be in a favourable position. In fact, the situation was desperate, especially for Austria, who was now eager to conclude a separate peace with the Entente. The full weakness of Austria–Hungary became clear in 1917–18, when the home front began to crack (**163**).

The nationalities and the war

The political history of Austria–Hungary in 1914–18 can only be understood against the background of military events (**154**). During the first half of the war the general feeling of the nationalities towards the Monarchy was one of loyalty. But among two groups – the Czechs and South Slavs – disaffection was evident, if not yet widespread. The Czechs pursued a policy of 'keeping an iron in every fire' (**15**). Most political leaders were pro-Habsburg: some sought the destruction of the Monarchy with Russian help; others, mostly émigrés, worked for an independent Czecho-Slovak state with Western help. At the popular level the Czechs were hostile to the monarchy. In April 1915 the 28th Prague Infantry Batallion deserted to the Russians and the Austrian authorities responded by arresting Karel Kramář, the Young Czech leader who looked to Russia for his country's salvation, and by combating the activities of the Czech underground organisation, the so-called Mafia (**163**). The most prominent Czech to go abroaad to persuade the world of the justice of the idea of Czech independence was Thomas Masaryk. With Kramar under arrest, Masaryk and his assistant, Edward Beneš were able gradually to persuade Czech politicians at home to accept the idea of seeking help from the Allied Powers and of including the Slovaks (who lived in Hungary) in an independent state. To this end he founded the Czecho-Slovak National Council in Paris in late 1916 (**158**).

The South Slavs, unlike the Czechs, could look to an existing independent country, Serbia, as the nucleus of a future Yugoslav state. Leading radicals, such as Mestrovic, Trumbić and Supilo, from the South Slav provinces of the Empire, decided very early in the war to go into exile and work for the unequivocal defeat and dissolution of the Monarchy. They formed the South Slav Committee in Paris in April 1915 and sought to convince the Allied politicians that the Habsburg Monarchy was 'an artificial and monstrous structure' (**163**). Among Croatians and Slovenes within the Empire, however, the émigrés' call went unheeded until the Declaration of Corfu (July 1917), which proclaimed the union of Serbs, Croats and Slovenes in a future Yugoslav state.

The ideas of the Slav émigrés found a ready echo in Britain among a group of sympathisers, led by the historian, R.W. Seton-Watson, and the *Times* journalist Wickham Steed. Both men had an inside knowledge of the Empire and in December 1916 they founded a weekly journal, the *New Europe*, which called for 'the emancipation of the subject races of central and south-eastern Europe from German and Magyar control' (**153**, **158**). Seton-Watson and Steed popularised the Slav national movements in Britain and put pressure on the Foreign Office to recognise that the Allied commitment to democracy and self determination entailed the break-up of the Monarchy. This was not the accepted view in the West at the time; rather, it was thought that national self-determination could be satisfied within a reorganised federal Habsburg Empire (**162**). But Masaryk, a frequent contributor to the *New Europe*, took a different view: 'Either the Habsburgs, or a free democratic Europe; that is the question. Any compromise between the two is bound to be an unstable condition' (**158**)

The *New Europe*, which ran from 1916 to 1922, was a brilliant journal full of insights into the world of east European politics and especially good on the danger of Pan-Germanism in the event of victory by the Central Powers. But as a guide to the events of the last two years of the war it is misleading because it exaggerates the role of the radicals in the break-up of the Monarchy. It is a mistake to pre-date the calls for the destruction of the Empire to the early, or even middle, years of the war. The Allied Powers had not committed themselves to the break-up of the Monarchy, nor had the forces of radical nationalism found a receptive audience among the people living inside Austria–Hungary until well into 1917 or 1918 (**152**).

1917 and 1918: military defeat and disintegration

The last two years of the war were crucial to the fate of the Habsburg Monarchy and it is to this period that we must look for the first rents in the imperial fabric. One of the most influential interpretations of the collapse of the Monarchy was put forth by Otto Bauer, the Social Democrat, in his book, *The Austrian Revolution* (1925). Bauer argued that the final collapse was brought about by two external events: the Russian Revolution in 1917 and the military defeat of Germany in 1918. According to Bauer, the Russian Revolution encouraged the national revolutions of the Poles, Czechs and Yugoslavs within the Dual Monarchy, and the defeat of the German Empire ensured the victory of these national revolutions (**151**). This view makes sense when one thinks of the Habsburg Monarchy as a bulwark, not against the Turkish Empire, which was a spent force, but against Russian Tsardom on one side and the German Empire on the other. When both these threats disappeared, the multinational Habsburg Empire lost its inner dynamic and broke into its national units.

Bauer's analysis stressed the vulnerability of the Habsburg Monarchy to external events, but tended to neglect developments within the Empire. The most important fact about the domestic political life of Austria was the adjournment of parliament from March 1914 to May 1917. The Reichsrat building was in fact turned into a hospital. Count Stürgkh, the prime minister, took this action because he feared that open discussion in parliament would lead to disloyal outbursts among the non-German representatives. Austria was ruled in an absolutist way, with many areas of life under military administration. One consequence of the suppression of freedom came in October 1916, when Victor Adler's son, Friedrich, assassinated Stürgkh in an act of defiance against the war regime. In the public trial which followed Adler turned his defence into an indictment of the government (**12**).

The second significant event to occur in the late months of 1916 was the death of Franz Joseph on 21 November 1916 in the 68th year of his reign. He was succeeded by his great-nephew, the 29-year-old Archduke Charles. One of the main aims of Charles' short reign was to obtain peace – along with Germany if possible, without Germany if necessary. To this end the two central Powers declared their readiness to enter into peace negotiations with the Entente powers in December 1916, but nothing came of these negotiations owing mainly to Germany's refusal to yield territory on the western front to France. The new Emperor then appointed the energetic Count Czernin as foreign minister in the hope of reaching an early peace. But Czernin refused to go too far in working for a separate peace with the Allies for fear of betraying the alliance with Germany and the ruling Austro-German and Magyar elites within the Empire. One set of peace negotiations was carried out between Austria and France in May 1917, without Czernin's knowledge, by Charles' brother-in-law, Prince Sixtus of Parma. Its importance lies not in the outcome, since it was abortive, but in the fact that one year later Clemenceau disclosed that Austria had supported France's 'just claims to Alsace-Lorraine' (**15**). The Sixtus affair damaged the Dual Alliance and revealed the extent to which Austria had become a satellite of Germany. In August 1918 Emperor Charles had to visit the German headquarters at Spa and publicly disown his independent peace policy (**12**).

The logical alternative to a separate peace for Austria was some measure of internal reform (e.g., federalism and the revival of parliament) which would break the German–Magyar stranglehold and galvanise the Slav peoples behind the war effort. Charles recognised the need for reform both in relations with Hungary and with regard to parliamentary government in Austria. Unfortunately, he did not use the occasion of his coronation in Hungary to force any changes in the Compromise of 1867. He passed up the opportunity to persuade Count Tisza, the Hungarian prime minister, and the Hungarian parliament to extend the franchise and grant some form of autonomy to the non-Magyar national groups. The failure to change the dualist arrangement with Hungary impeded all schemes for Slav autonomy, as Franz Ferdinand had clearly seen before 1914. This must be reckoned one of the fundamental causes of the break-up of the Habsburg Monarchy (**21**, **156**, **162**).

Emperor Charles was eager to appear as a constitutional monarch and in May 1917 he allowed the parliament to be reconvened after three years of absolutist rule. It is interesting to note that at the meeting of the Reichsrat only a few isolated members called for the dissolution of the Monarchy. The overwhelming majority of Czechs, South Slavs and Ruthenes wanted reorganisation of the Monarchy as a federal state guaranteeing the autonomy of the national groups (**163**). At this stage of the war the radical ideas of the Slav émigrés and their sympathisers on the board of the *New Europe* had not become the accepted view of Slav politicians at home (**154**). Meanwhile, two events in the early months of 1917 – the Russian Revolution and the entry of the United States into the war – changed the Allies' policy towards the Central Powers.

More important than either the Sixtus affair or the recall of the parliament was the March Revolution in Russia in 1917 (followed by the Bolshevik Revolution in November), which brought down the Tsarist government. If the absolutist government in Russia could be brought down so easily, was the absolutist government safe in Austria? In Z.A.B. Zeman's words, 'the spectre of revolution began to haunt the rulers of the Danube monarchy' (**163**). The summoning of the parliament was a response to the threat. Under the impact of the Russian Revolution a group of radical Czech authors outside parliament issued a 'Manifesto' calling for the first time for an independent Czecho-Slovak state. In the winter of 1917–18 there was a severe food crisis, flour was rationed in Vienna and a strike movement spread to all the industrial districts of Austria. In March Czech prisoners of war, began returning from Russia carrying Bolshevik ideas. Yet in spite of widespread disaffection among the subjects of the Habsburg Monarchy in early 1918 a Bolshevik-type revolution did not occur. Why? The reason is that unrest was diverted into national channels and hence the revolutionary movement took the form of a struggle for independence by the various nationalities (**163**).

The United States entered the war in April 1917, one month after the first Russian Revolution. These two events injected a strong ideological element into the war. The Allies, now rid of the incubus of Tsarist absolutism, could openly support the democratic national movements within the Habsburg Monarchy. But it must be remembered that the entry of the United States did not by itself signal the break-up of the Monarchy (**151**). Point 10 of President Wilson's 14 Points (January 1918) called for the reorganisation of the Danubian Monarchy, not its disintegration: 'The peoples of Austria–Hungary, whose place among the nations we wish to see safeguarded and assured, should be accorded the freest opportunity for autonomous development' (**154**).

It was military considerations which finally persuaded the Allies to push for the break-up of the Monarchy. The decision was made in the spring of 1918, when the Germans launched their offensive in the West. It now became clear that Austria–Hungary would not detach herself from the Dual Alliance, and so the Allies pursued a policy of encouraging the nationalist movements within the Empire (**151**).

In the early months of 1918 the Czech, Pole and South Slav

politicians inside the Empire began calling for its disintegration. In the summer the Allied Powers followed suit. In September 1918 they recognised the right of the Czechoslovaks to independence. The position of the Czechs was crucial because, unlike the Poles and South Slavs who could look to national centres outside the Empire, the creation of a Czech state would inevitably entail the break-up of the Habsburg Monarchy (**163**).

The failure of the German offensive in the West and the failure of an Austrian offensive against Italy in June 1918 sealed the fate of the Empire (**160**). In September, Bulgaria sued for peace and in early October Austria, Germany and Turkey appealed to President Wilson for an armistice on the basis of the 14 Points. Meanwhile, a final effort was made by Minister President Max Hussarek on 16 October to reconstruct the Monarchy into a federal state. It came too late and provided instead 'a basis for the liquidation of the monarchy' (**151**). On 27 October a cabinet under Professor Lammasch was set up to carry out precisely this task. By the end of the month the Czechs and Yugoslavs had proclaimed their independence, followed by the Magyars and Poles a few days later. On 11 November 1918 Emperor Charles abdicated. The Habsburg Monarchy had ceased to exist.

Part Four: Assessment

The collapse of the Austro-Hungarian Empire in 1918 has not ended speculation about the Habsburg 'mission' and the reasons for its decline and fall. Nor have historians alone had a monopoly on these speculations. Two famous books – Joseph Roth's *Radetzkymarsch* (1932) and Rebecca West's *Black Lamb and Grey Falcon* (1942), the first a novel, the second a travel book – brilliantly portray, from opposing standpoints, the Habsburg Monarchy in its death throes.

In *Radetzkymarsch* the fall of the Empire is mirrored in the story of the Trotta family over three generations (**126**). The novel opens with the elevation of Lieutenant Joseph Trotta to the nobility as a reward for saving the life of the young Emperor Franz Joseph at the battle of Solferino in 1859. A tradition of imperial service is thus established: the son becomes a district officer (*Bezirkshauptmann*) of a remote province and the grandson, Carl Joseph, joins the army. The story focuses on Carl Joseph and his inability to adjust to the duties and traditions of army life. Through the fortunes of the Trotta family Roth charts the decline in values, especially military values, which accompanied the decline of the Empire.

Thus while the grandfather is portrayed as saving the Emperor's life by a supreme act of heroism, the grandson is shown as incapable of doing more than rescue a portrait of Franz Joseph from a brothel. Roth did not idealise the old monarchy in this novel, but there is a sense of regret over the loss of a world which never questioned its basic values and beliefs. When Hitler came to power in Germany the author went into exile in Paris where he became a monarchist and apologist for the old Habsburg supranational state (**103**).

Rebecca West's *Black Lamb and Grey Falcon* is based on a journey the author took through Yugoslavia in 1937. It is not so much a conventional travel book as a penetrating study of the history of the Balkan peoples. Although only part of the book is devoted to the Habsburg Empire, it contains a withering indictment of 'the scar on the Slav peoples' left by Austrian rule (**31**). For Rebecca West the Habsburgs were at their worst in their relations with the alien races of the Empire and the murder of Franz Ferdinand in Sarajevo was only the logical consequence of a long period of misrule over the South Slavs. *Black Lamb and Grey Falcon* belongs to the English radical tradition, stretching from Gladstone in the nineteenth century to A.J.P. Taylor in our own day, which sees nothing good in the Habsburg Monarchy and whose sympathies lie with the subject Slav peoples.

Myths about the Habsburg Monarchy as a happy cosmopolitan union of peoples, or conversely as a 'peoples' prison', first sprang up in the nineteenth century and have been cultivated by imaginative writers and historians ever since (**23**). For the historian, the Habsburg Monarchy is a subject of great importance because of the strategic position it occupied in central and eastern Europe from 1867 to 1918. The crucial question of the period was that of nationalism. Both within the Empire and on its periphery the bitter conflict between the new cause of nationalism and the old principle of dynastic imperialism was fought out.

There is a temptation among historians to take a western European view towards nationalism and assume that the eleven national groups within the Austro–Hungarian Empire would sooner or later have achieved autonomous statehood. But few people living in western or eastern Europe in the late nineteenth and early twentieth centuries envisaged such an outcome. Even Karl Marx, who could not be accused of bourgeois sympathies, thought that the Slavs (Poles excepted), as a people without an independent national history, would and should remain under the more 'progressive' rule of the Germans and Magyars (**11**). The races were so mixed in many parts of eastern Europe that it was impossible to untie the knot simply by re-drawing the map along national boundaries. The Czechs were not the only peoples who wanted more privileges for themselves rather than the dissolution of the monarchy. The question at issue, therefore, was how much autonomy should be granted to national groups within the Empire. This was a matter of degree and compromise which did not touch the fundamental question of the Monarchy's existence.

The nationality question stands at the centre of the historical controversy over the causes of the downfall of the Habsburg Monarchy. One school of interpretation, led by Oscar Jászi, sees the fall of the monarchy as an 'organic' process caused by internal contradictions and failure to solve the nationality problems (**10**). Jászi's classic study, *The Dissolution of the Habsburg Monarchy* (1929), shows how the centripetal forces at work in the Empire – the dynasty, army, aristocracy, Catholic Church, bureaucracy and capitalism –

ultimately succumbed to the more dynamic, centrifugal force of nationalism. He argues convincingly that the nationality issue was never treated by the Habsburg rulers as a fundamental problem, but only as a matter of tactics. A 'reasonable federalism' would have solved it, but this was never achieved because of opposition from Hungary. For Jászi the Austrian ship of state foundered on the rock of dualism.

An opposite interpretation of the downfall of the Habsburg Monarchy, put forward by Hans Kohn, Hugo Hantsch and Edward Crankshaw, traces the cause of collapse to World War One, not to the nationality conflict (**4**, **9**, **155**). These historians see foreign-policy decisions as crucial to the fate of the Monarchy. The great power policy of the Habsburgs, in particular the occupation and annexation of Bosnia and Herzegovina in 1878 and 1908 respectively, led to the fatal antagonism with Russia. The decisive blow came in World War One, when the Austro–Hungarian Empire proved unable by itself to defeat its enemies on all sides, Russia, Serbia and Italy. In Crankshaw's words, the Monarchy collapsed 'because it lost a war to people who hated dynasties' (**4**).

Either interpretation, taken by itself, seems to me one–sided. Why treat them as opposites? The nationality question and the war were inextricably linked problems, as I hope the previous chapters have made clear. It may be true that foreign affairs were the deciding factor in shaping the Monarchy during the period of constitutional experiments from 1848 to 1867. A.J.P. Taylor expressed the view that 'the fate of the Habsburg Monarchy had been decided by the war of 1866' (**21**). By this he meant that Franz Joseph had to accept a dualist constitution in 1867 (which established Magyar hegemony in Hungary and Austro–German hegemony in Austria) in order to preserve the Empire. Put another way, Austria–Hungary could only continue as a great power by keeping the majority Slav population in permanent subjection. Taylor went on to argue that in her foreign policy Austria–Hungary was never able to escape from German domination after 1867 and that the defeat and dissolution of the Monarchy in 1918 was the logical consequence of her dependence on her defeated ally, Germany.

Taylor's thesis has a compelling logic about it, but in the final analysis it is too deterministic and discounts the impact of internal structure on foreign policy. After 1867 the interplay of foreign and domestic policy had a different pattern from before. It is possible to identify six crucial political events – three domestic, three foreign – which mark the path to destruction:

1. 1871 – The failure to meet the Czech demands to change the Austrian half of the Empire into a federal state.

2. 1878 – The joint Austro-Hungarian occupation of Bosnia and Herzegovina.

3. 1879 – The Dual Alliance between Austria–Hungary and Germany.

4. 1897 – The failure of the Badeni language decrees, which would have put Czech and German on an equal basis in Bohemia; the effective end of parliamentary government in Austria.

5. 1906 – The failure of Franz Joseph to impose universal suffrage on Hungary and thereby end the Magyar stranglehold on the Slav peoples.

6. 1908 – The annexation of Bosnia and Herzegovina, which made Serbia and Russia into irreconcilable enemies of the Empire.

None of these events led logically to the next one, but each was a turning point which further closed the options available to the Habsburg rulers. It is impossible, for example, to disentangle Austria–Hungary's failure to solve the internal problems of South Slav nationalism in the two annexed provinces, Bosnia and Herzegovina, from the foreign-policy problem of a hostile Serbia backed by Russia. The annexation of the two provinces in 1908 exacerbated the internal nationalist problems, which in turn made it difficult for the Habsburg rulers to respond imaginatively to the assassination of Franz Ferdinand. In both foreign and domestic affairs the Habsburg rulers slowly boxed themselves into a corner during the two generations before 1914.

The fact of the Habsburg Monarchy's collapse in 1918 has inevitably coloured historians' views of its last years. It has often been treated as a doomed relic from around the year 1900. But it is worth remembering that even radical, contemporary critics such as Masaryk, Seton-Watson and Wickham Steed, who advocated the break-up of the Empire during World War One, had not pronounced its doom before 1914. Writing in 1913, Wickham Steed declared that the internal crises of the Empire were 'crises of growth rather than of decay' (**19**).

The habit of viewing the Monarchy as doomed before its actual end was common among the Viennese intelligentsia at the turn of the century. The image of the Monarchy as decadent and disintegrating owes much to the imaginative works of writers such as Robert Musil and Karl Kraus. It may, of course, be true that an intuitive feeling of impending crisis among the intellectual elite was also the very source of their creativity. As we have seen, there was a tendency among writers and artists in Vienna to escape into the private world of their imagination because they felt excluded from public life (**97**). The fascination with the irrational, which fuelled the destructive mass movements of the twentieth century, also inspired the revolution in the arts. The Vienna of Hitler's youth was also a cultural capital of Europe. The historian need not accept the artist's view of the world as the whole truth, but Karl Kraus uttered a true prophecy when he called Austria–Hungary in World War One a ' research laboratory for world destruction'.

Part Five: Documents

document 1

The nationalities of the Habsburg Monarchy

The following statistics indicate the relative strength (in percentages) of the different nationalities in each half of the Empire in Bosnia–Herzegovina and in the Empire as a whole.

OFFICIAL NATIONALITY STATISTICS (%)

	1880	1890	1900	1910
Cisleithanian Austria				
Germans	36.8	36.1	35.8	35.6
Czechs (incl. Slovaks)	23.8	23.3	23.2	23.0
Poles	14.9	15.8	16.6	17.8
Ruthenians	12.8	13.2	13.2	12.6
Serbo-Croats	2.6	2.8	2.8	2.6
Rumanians	0.9	0.9	0.9	1.0
Lands of the Hungarian Crown including Croatia–Slavonia				
Magyars	41.2	42.8	45.4	48.1
Germans	12.5	12.2	11.1	9.8
Slovaks	11.9	11.1	10.5	9.4
Rumanians	15.4	14.9	14.5	14.1
Ruthenians	2.3	2.2	2.2	2.3
Croats	—	9.0	8.7	8.8
Serbs	—	6.1	5.5	5.3
Bosnia–Herzegovina (estimates of 1910)				
Croats				21
Serbs				42
Mohammedans				34

Empire totals of 1910

Germans	23.9
Magyars	20.2
Czechs	12.6
Slovaks	3.8 (est.)
Croats	5.3
Serbs	3.8
Mohammedan Serbo-Croats in Bosnia–Herzegovina	1.2 (est.)
Poles	10.0
Ruthenians	7.9
Rumanians	6.4
Slovenes	2.6
Italians	2.0

R.A. Kann, (**12**), pp. 606–7.

document 2

The nationalities of the Czech lands in 1900

	Nationality	*Percentage of population*
Bohemia	Czechs	62.68
	Germans	37.26
	Others	0.06
Moravia	Czechs	71.36
	Germans	27.90
	Poles	0.65
	Others	0.09
Silesia	Germans	44.69
	Poles	33.21
	Czechs	22.04
	Others	0.06

P. Vyšný, (**79**), p.3.

document 3
Index of Austrian industrial production, 1880–1913 (1900=100)

Year	Index	Year	Index
1880	44	1897	91
1881	49	1898	98
1882	51	1899	99
1883	57	1900	100
1884	59	1901	105
1885	56	1902	105
1886	60	1903	106
1887	62	1904	107
1888	61	1905	113
1889	66	1906	118
1890	72	1907	135
1891	77	1908	132
1892	78	1909	129
1893	80	1910	130
1894	86	1911	137
1895	89	1912	150
1896	90	1913	144

R.L. Rudolph, (**56**), p. 19.

document 4
The share of different countries in European and world trade, 1860–1908 (%)

Country	Share of European trade			Share of world trade		
	1860	1870	1880	1885	1895	1908
Great Britain	33.4	33.4	30.4	19.2	17.8	17.2
France	17.5	16.5	17.6	10.4	8.6	8.9
Germany	16.8	15.4	15.4	10.3	11.1	12.3
Russia	4.8	7.3	5.1	5.6	6.0	3.0
Austria–Hungary	5.4	6.0	7.2	3.7	3.7	3.3

A. Wandruszka, vol.1, (**23**), p. 19.

document 5

Steel production and consumption: different countries, 1880–1913

Country	Steel production (1,000 tons)			Steel production, per capita (tons)	
	1891	*1901*	*1911*	*1893/97*	*1903/07*
Great Britain	3,157	4,897	6,565	0.09	0.14
France	744	1,425	3,837	0.02	0.06
Germany	2,563	6,211	14,556	0.08	0.16
Russia	429	2,212	3,933	0.007	0.014
Austria–Hungary	486	1,142	2,327	0.017	0.024
Belgium	244	530	2,193	0.07	0.24

A. Wandruszka, vol, 1, (**23**), p. 26.

document 6

Index of Hungarian harvest yields, 1871–1915

Years	Wheat	Rye	Barley	Oats	Maize	Potatoes	Sugar beets	Turnips
1871–75	100	100	100	100	100	100	100	100
1876–80	154	113	126	132	174	181	195	247
1881–85	222	141	158	153	214	301	271	497
1886–90	261	142	150	149	201	282	333	627
1891–95	309	156	184	185	274	338	571	852
1896–1900	269	141	180	190	267	440	664	1,000
1901–05	315	167	189	200	229	482	784	1,123
1905–11	315	163	206	211	358	555	1,038	1,537
1911–15	316	163	227	229	365	615	1,577	1,643

A. Wandruszka, vol. 1, (**23**), p. 422.

document 7

Distribution of national income in Austria by area, 1911–13

Region	Share (%)	Average per capita income (crowns)	Population (%) (1910)
Austria (Upper and Lower)	33.8	790	26
Czech lands (Bohemia, Moravia, Silesia)	42.8	630	36
Galicia	13.7	250	28
South Tirol, Trieste, Istria	4.7	450	5
Slovenia, Dalmatia	3.3	300	3
Bukovina	1.6	300	2

R.L. Rudolph, (**56**), p. 19.

document 8

Parliamentary riots in Austria in 1897

*The American writer, Mark Twain, was in Vienna when the Badeni govern-
ment introduced two language decrees in parliament which intended to put the
Czech language on an equal footing with German in the provinces of Bohemia
and Moravia. From the public gallery he witnessed the riots which effectively
ended parliamentary government in Austria.*

And now we see what history will be talking of five centuries hence:
a uniformed and helmeted battalion of bronzed and stalwart men
marching in double file down the floor of the House – a free parliament profaned by an invasion of brute force!

It was an odious spectacle – odious and aweful. For one moment it
was an unbelievable thing – a thing beyond all credibility; it must
be a delusion, a dream, a nightmare. But no, it was real – pitifully
real, shamefully real, hideously real. These sixty policemen had
been soldiers, and they went at their work with the cold unsen-
timentality of their trade. They ascended the steps of the tribune,
laid their hands upon the inviolable persons of the representatives of
a nation, and dragged and tugged them down the steps and out at
the door: then ranged themselves in stately military array in front of
the ministerial estrade and so stood.

Some of the results of this wild freak followed instantly. The
Badeni government came down with a crash; there was a popular
outbreak or two in Vienna: there were three or four days of furious
rioting in Prague, followed by the establishing there of martial law;
the Jews and Germans were harried and plundered and their houses
destroyed; in other Bohemian towns there was rioting – in some
cases the Germans being the rioters, in others the Czechs – and in all
cases the Jew had to roast, no matter which side he was on. We are
well along in December now; the new Minister–President has not
been able to patch up a peace among the warring factions of the
parliament, therefore there is no use in calling it together again for
the present; public opinion believes that parliamentary government
and the Constitution are actually threatened with extinction, and
that the permanency of the monarchy itself is a not absolutely
certain thing!

M. Twain, 'Stirring Times in Austria', *Harper's New Monthly Maga-
zine* (1897), p. 540.

document 9
Leon Trotsky's impressions of the Austrian socialists

Trotsky lived in Vienna from 1907 to 1914. He found the Austrian Marxists too academic and said that life in Austria reminded him too much of a 'squirrel in a cage'.

In October, 1907 I was already in Vienna ... It was Hilferding who first introduced me to his friends in Vienna, Otto Bauer, Max Adler, and Karl Renner. They were well-educated people whose knowledge of various subjects was superior to mine. I listened with intense and, one might almost say, respectful interest to their conversation in the 'Central' café. But very soon I grew puzzled. These people were not revolutionaries. Moreover, they represented the type that was furthest from that of the revolutionary. This expressed itself in everything – in their approach to subjects, in their political remarks and psychological appreciations, in their self-satisfaction – not self-assurance, but self-satisfaction. I even thought I sensed philistinism in the quality of their voices.

I was surprised to find that these educated Marxists were absolutely incapable of applying Marx's method as soon as they came to the big problems of politics, especially its revolutionary turns.

In the old imperial, hierarchic, vain and futile Vienna, the academic Marxists would refer to each other with a sort of sensuous delight as 'Herr Doktor'. Workers often called the academicians, 'Genosse Herr Doktor'. During all the seven years that I lived in Vienna, I never had a heart-to-heart talk with any one of this upper group, although I was a member of the Austrian Social Democracy, attended their meetings, took part in their demonstrations, contributed to their publications, and sometimes made short speeches in German. I felt that the leaders of the Social Democrats were alien, whereas I found, quite easily, a mutual language with the Social Democratic workers at meetings or at May Day demonstrations.

L. Trotsky, *My Life* Butterworth, 1930, pp. 213–15.

document 10
The self-image of the Jews in Central Europe

George Clare's book, Last Waltz in Vienna. The Destruction of a Family, 1842–1942 *(1981), traces the fortunes of his own Jewish family, the*

Klaars, over three generations. This extract illustrates the sensitivity of the assimilated Jew to his position in society.

I was happily kneeling on the polished wooden bench of a river steamer a few hours later, looking out over the glittering water. Everything was lovely – until the moment when I turned round to ask Father a question. Then disaster – and Father – struck for the second time that day. I had begun my question with the words: '*Tate*, what is...?' I felt a stinging slap on my right cheek. Father had hit me again. 'Don't you ever dare to call me *Tate*,' he hissed, 'never, you hear, never!' I have no idea what suddenly possessed me to call him *Tate*, to use the Yiddish word for 'Father', instead of the usual 'Daddy' or 'Papa'. I must have picked it up somewhere.

That brief and ugly scene, over in less than a minute, encapsulated the entire conflict dividing Central European Jewry. We, the Klaars, already belonged to the worldly Jews with Western European education and culture. We wore fine clothes, had access even to titles and dignities, possessed influence and wealth. But full equality, inner equality, still eluded us. It eluded not only those who like us had retained our Jewish faith, however spuriously we practised it, but even those who had gone the whole way and converted. We knew that the others, the *Goyim*, however polite or even servile, did not really differentiate between the caftaned Yiddish speaker with the long wobbling side-curls and the smoothly shaven elegant, à la Klaar, from the Viennese coffee-houses.

And perhaps we, the grandchildren and great-grandchildren, also subconsciously envied those strange alien creatures from the east, for they possessed something that we, the coffee-house elegants steeped in German culture, had lost: a strong religious conviction with its belief in a divinely ordained future. This enabled them to bear lowly social status and prejudice with equanimity, while we trembled at the slightest sign of discrimination.

G. Clare, (**28**), p. 85.

document 11
The impact of Vienna on young Adolf Hitler

Hitler lived as a young man in Vienna from 1908 to 1913. He failed the entrance examination into the Academy of Art, worked on temporary jobs and drifted in and out of men's hostels. Here he acquired his first political education.

Hitler detested Vienna as the capital of a multi-racial empire, but the Christian Social Party and the Pan-German movement made a great impact on him.

In those days I followed both movements most attentively. One, by feeling the beat of its innermost heart, the other, carried away by admiration for the unusual man who even then seemed to me a bitter symbol of all Austrian Germanism.

When the mighty funeral procession bore the dead mayor from the City Hall towards the Ring, I was among the many hundred thousands looking on at the tragic spectacle. I was profoundly moved and my feelings told me that the work, even of this man, was bound to be in vain, owing to the fatal destiny which would inevitably lead this state to destruction. If Dr. Karl Lueger had lived in Germany, he would have been ranked among the great minds of our people; that he lived and worked in this impossible state was the misfortune of his work and of himself ...

If, in addition to its enlightened knowledge of the broad masses, the Christian Social Party had had a correct idea of the importance of the racial question, such as the Pan-German movement had achieved; and if, finally, it had itself been nationalistic, or if the Pan-German movement, in addition to its correct knowledge of the aim of the Jewish question, had adopted the practical shrewdness of the Christian Social Party, especially in its attitude towards socialism, there would have resulted a movement which even then in my opinion might have successfully intervened in German destiny ...

I was repelled by the conglomeration of races which the capital showed me, repelled by this whole mixture of Czechs, Poles, Hungarians, Ruthenians, Serbs, and Croats, and everywhere, the eternal mushroom of humanity – Jews and more Jews.

To me the giant city seemed the embodiment of racial desecration ... Yet Vienna was and remained for me the hardest, though most thorough, school of my life. I had set foot in this town while still a boy and I left it a man, grown quiet and grave. In it I obtained the foundations for a philosophy in general and a political view in particular which later I only needed to supplement in detail, but which never left me.

A. Hitler, *Mein Kampf* (English edition, Hutchinson 1974), pp. 111–14.

document 12

Vienna as a 'Jewish city'

*The disproportionately large role played by the Jewish population in Vienna in
almost every sphere of life is described by the socialist leader, Julius Braunthal,
in his autobiography,* In Search of the Millenium *(1945).*

It would certainly be a gross exaggeration to say that Vienna was
ever a 'Jewish city'; it was one of the finest German cities, with a rich
heritage of German culture, strongly moulded in music and
architecture by Italian influence; only one in ten of its population
was of Jewish descent. Yet though the Jewish population of Vienna
was comparatively small in numbers – about 200,000 out of two
millions – the Jewish thread in the economic, social and above all,
the spiritual fabric of Vienna was very conspicuous, perhaps even
more than in the fabric of New York or Warsaw ... At any rate, the
Jews achieved in Vienna greater eminence, for good and for evil,
than anywhere else in Europe, an eminence in all walks of economic
life, and in letters, science, music, and especially in the Socialist
movement. In the invigorating air of this remarkable cosmopolis,
where the culture of the European West met with that of the European East and blended with it, the Jewish talent blossomed as
vigorously as it did in Granada under Moslem rule. The old-world
culture which they had retained and developed in the medieval
setting of Eastern Europe underwent amazing processes of meta-
morphosis in Vienna, processes in the course of which the Jews
themselves changed in mind and behaviour and in turn influenced
their new environment perceptibly. The peculiar character of the
Austrian Labour movement – for example, its astonishing blend of
enthusiastic Messianism and sober Fabianism, of revolutionary
Marxism and reformist Trade Unionism – was produced, in the first
place by particular historic conditions; but it was also the result of
the blending of the German and Jewish elements which composed it.

J. Braunthal, (**27**), pp. 16–17.

document 13

Art in Vienna in 1902

*The hostess and author, Berta Szeps, knew most of Vienna's artists and writers
in the early twentieth century. Here she describes a poignant meeting between
Gustav Klimt and the French artist, Rodin.*

When Rodin came to Vienna in 1902 to visit the wonderful exhibition held by the Sezession and dedicated to sculpture, I took him to see Klimt ...

My husband and I had asked Rodin to a real Viennese 'Jause' (afternoon coffee). It was a wonderful June afternoon in the Prater, and all the Sezessionists had assembled there. Klimt was in a brilliant mood and sat next to Rodin, who talked enthusiastically to him about the beauties of Vienna.

I had coffee served on the terrace. Klimt and Rodin had seated themselves beside two remarkably beautiful young women – Rodin gazing enchantedly at them. Klimt had created an ideal of this type – the 'modern' woman, with a boyish slimness and a puzzling charm. The expression 'vamp' had not yet enriched our vocabularies, but it was Klimt who first invented or discovered the ideal Garbo or Dietrich long before Hollywood had stamped those figures upon the dreams of young men all over the world. And, that afternoon, slim and lovely vamps came buzzing round Klimt and Rodin, those two fiery lovers. Alfred Gruenfeld sat down at the piano in the big drawing-room, whose double doors were opened wide. Klimt went up to him and asked, 'Please play us some Schubert.' And Gruenfeld, his cigar in his mouth, played dreamy tunes that floated and hung in the air with the smoke of his cigar.

Rodin leaned over to Klimt and said: 'I have never before experienced such an atmosphere – your tragic and magnificent Beethoven fresco; your unforgettable, temple-like exhibition; and now this garden, these women, this music ... and round it all this gay, child-like happiness ... What is the reason for it all?'

And Klimt slowly nodded his beautiful head and answered only one word – 'Austria.'

B. Szeps, *My Life and History*, Cassell and Co., 1938, pp. 144–45.

document 14
The occupation of Bosnia and Herzegovina, 1878

Adolf Fischhof, a leader of the Vienna revolution of 1848, clearly foresaw the dangers for the future of the eastern policy of Franz Joseph and Andrássy. He made the following prediction in a private letter written at the time of the annexation of Bosnia and Herzegovina.

What do you think of the position Austria owes to the cleverness of its Andrássy? A sound eastern policy is possible only on the basis of a rational domestic policy, non-injurious to the Slav peoples, since the eastern question is a predominantly Slav one. Panslavism could have been overcome by the opposition, to it, of a sound idea: not by mobilizing a great army. The Panslav bait could have been put out of action by reasonable encouragement to Slav particularism. But an Austria which repels its own Slavs has no attractive force for Slavs and Turks. That makes a good and successful eastern policy impossible. But there are graduations in evil and, in our good old Austrian way, we have busily promoted the most evil and the most stupid possible result for ourselves.

Andrássy is our political Benedek. Wrapped in the fog of his own *idée fixe*, like the fog that surrounded his unhappy countryman at Chlum, he was surrounded and taken in the rear, without so much as knowing it. And this diplomatic defeat now is far more momentous in its consequences than military disaster was then, for while the latter reduced our might the former threatens our very existence ... In the long run it is not an alliance of princes, nor an entente cordiale of diplomats that is going to help us, but unity at home and the friendly co-operation of all the nationalities that make up our state, for the chasm that divides our nationalities will one day be the grave of the monarchy

Quoted in Redlich, (**17**), pp. 395–96.

document 15
The Dual Alliance between Austria–Hungary and Germany, 1879

The Dual Alliance was the foundation stone of Austrian foreign policy from 1879 to 1918. The main articles of the treaty are given below.

ARTICLE I
Should, contrary to their hope, and against the loyal desire of the two High Contracting Parties, one of the two Empires be attacked by Russia, the High Contracting Parties are bound to come to the assistance one of the other with the whole war strength of their Empires, and accordingly only to conclude peace together and upon mutual agreement.

ARTICLE II
Should one of the High Contracting Parties be attacked by another Power, the other High Contracting Party binds itself hereby, not

only not to support the aggressor against its high Ally, but to observe at least a benevolent neutral attitude towards its fellow Contracting Party.

Should, however, the attacking party in such a case be supported by Russia, either by an active cooperation or by military measures which constitute a menace to the Party attacked, then the obligation stipulated in Article I of this Treaty, for reciprocal assistance with the whole fighting force, becomes equally operative ...

ARTICLE III
The duration of this Treaty shall be provisionally fixed at five years from the day of ratification.

ARTICLE IV
This Treaty shall, in conformity with its peaceful character, and to avoid any misinterpretation, be kept secret by the two High Contracting Parties, and only communicated to a third Power upon a joint understanding between the two Parties, and according to the terms of a special Agreement.

A. Pribram, (**147**), pp. 27–29.

document 16
Aehrenthal's proposed solution to the South Slav problem

As Austrian foreign minister Aehrenthal won notoriety as the man responsible for the unilateral Habsburg annexation of Bosnia and Herzegovina in 1908. But in two unpublished memoirs written in 1907, he revealed his positive, long-range plans to solve the South Slav problem.

The problem of preparing a favourable formation of relations on the southern border of the Monarchy in the event of a collapse of Turkish rule had been ... for the time being negatively construed by Count Andrássy. The influence of the Monarchy was thrown into the balance to prevent the formation of an unfavourable constellation; until now we have avoided formulating a positive concept to provide for the future development of things in a sense favourable to us. For decades our policy concerning the southern frontier had adhered to this negative standpoint. Externally, it was characterised by the proclamation of the *status quo*, which made a closer attachment of the occupied provinces impossible, while internally we did not succeed in grouping the Slavonic elements in the south of the Monarchy in a manner which would have made them a counterbalance to the strong attraction of the Great-Serbian idea emanating from Belgrade.

[In order effectively to further the Monarchy's interests in the southern regions, Aehrenthal proposed that a real South Slav group consisting of Croatia, Slavonia and Dalmatia, with Agram (Zagreb) as its centre, should be created within the Hungarian half of the monarchy. He asserted that a strong South Slav group ...]

... will in the long run, lead not to a strengthening of the *Magyar concept*, but will lead the Monarchy onto that road which is perhaps the most suitable to her development: The road to Trialism.

Quoted in S. Wank, (**146**), pp. 519–21.

document 17
South Slavs inside and outside the Habsburg Monarchy

The following tables, based on calculations made by R.W. Seton-Watson before 1914, show that twice as many South Slavs lived inside the Monarchy as outside it.

TABLE XVII

Jugo-Slavs inside the Habsburg Monarchy (in round numbers)	
I. In Austria (Carniola, Carinthia, Styria, Istria, Dalmatia)	
a) Slovenes	1,400,000
b) Croats	700,000
c) Serbs	100,000
II. In Hungary	
a) Croats	300,000
b) Serbs	500,000
III. In Croatia–Slavonia	
a) Croats	1,750,000
b) Serbs	650,000
IV. Bosnia–Herzegovina	
a) Croats	400,000
b) Serbs	850,000
c) Mohammedan Serbo-Croats	650,000
Total	7,300,000

TABLE XVIII

Jugo-Slavs outside the Habsburg Monarchy	
I. In Serbia	2,600,000
II. In Montenegro	300,000
III. In Turkey	400,000
Total	3,300,000

Quoted in O. Jászi (**10**), p. 405.

document 18
Relations between Serbia and Austria-Hungary

Dr Joseph Baernreither, a prominent member of the Upper House and an expert on the South Slav problem, tried for years to bridge the gap between Serbia and Austria. In this extract from his memoirs, Fragments of a Political Diary *(1930), he describes his failure to bring together Aehrenthal and the Serbian foreign minister, Milovanovic, in 1910.*

I warmly expressed the convictions I had so often put out in full and in vain in the Delegation. The centre of gravity of the Serbo-Croat world must be placed within the Monarchy, and, within it, must be guaranteed freedom of self-development; the policy of annexation must be followed up by a policy of attraction; our whole South Slav policy, both external and internal, must be fundamentally changed. Once again, however, I experienced disappointment. Aehrenthal seemed to be more or less familiar with the run of Milovanovic's ideas, but described them as the music of the future ...

He [Aehrenthal] saw quite well that the Balkan situation demanded a new South Slav policy and a new attitude to Serbia on our part, but at the same time he was tied by the tail to Germany's Eastern policy. And, for him, this last was plainly at once more actual and more urgent; any change in our South Slav policy would bring him into collision with the selfish and short-sighted agrarian policy of Hungary, nor could he count on any support from the German parties in Austria, who simply did not understand Balkan politics. Therefore he did not throw himself whole-heartedly into either of the two courses. In Balkan politics, so he observed to me shortly after, two turns are necessary – one with Germany for Turkey, another for the Slav peoples. Our South Slav policy was to be wrecked on this game ...

If the Monarchy had been able to give the Serbian people something to look forward to ... the course of events in the Balkans would in all probability have been wholly different from what it actually proved.

J. Baernreither, (**25**), pp. 91–95.

document 19

The Habsburg administration of Bosnia–Herzegovina, 1878–1908

The Habsburg record of administration in Bosnia and Herzegovina after 1878 was hotly debated by contemporaries. Heinrich Lammasch, Austria's last prime minister for two weeks in 1918, wrote a defence of his country's occupation of Bosnia and Herzegovina in a letter to the Times, *dated 10 November 1908.*

From the beginning our occupation of Bosnia was intended to be permanent, as for the benefit of Egypt your occupation of the Land of the Pyramids will prove to be permanent. In appreciation of these circumstances I believe I am justified in saying that the proclamation, dated 7 October 1908, has changed nothing in the world of reality of things, that it has put an end only to a mere fiction, and that therefore it is not in contradiction with the spirit of the Berlin Treaty. Turkey has lost nothing; on the contrary, it has regained, in consequence of the withdrawal of our troops out of the territory of Novi Bazar, the unlimited exercise of sovereignty in these regions.

And Servia? Servia complains that her aspirations to extend in times to come her dominion over Bosnia and Herzegovina have been checked by their formal incorporation in our monarchy. But can Servia claim any right to these territories? Nominally they belonged to Turkey, really to Austria–Hungary, but in no way at all to Servia. It is true that the inhabitants of these provinces are to a great extent of the same nationality as the Servians; but the greater part of them are not of the same religious persuasion as the Servians; they are either Catholics or Mahomedans, but not Orthodox. And in Eastern Europe religion is almost more the ground-work of the political configuration than nationality ...

If finally, we ask whether the Austro-Hungarian dominion or the Servian dominion would be more for the benefit of the inhabitants of . these regions, the answer can hardly be doubtful. The work Austria–Hungary has done these 30 years in the occupied territories has been

Documents

99

recognized throughout the world. When Mr. Holls, the American delegate to the first Hague Conference, came to Europe to study the administration of Bosnia as a model for that of the Philippine Islands and of Porto Rico, he acknowledged that Lord Cromer's administration in Egypt and Baron Kállay's administration in Bosnia were the best types of colonial government.

Extract from S. Verosta, *Theorie und Realität von Bundnissen*, Europa Verlag, 1971, p. 593.

Bibliography

GENERAL ACCOUNTS

1 Benedikt, H., *Die Monarchie des Hauses Österreich*, Verlag für Geschichte und Politik, 1968.
2 Borkenau, F., *Austria and After*, Faber and Faber, 1938.
3 Coxe, W., *History of the House of Austria*, 4 vols. G. Bell, 1895.
4 Crankshaw, E., *The Fall of the House of Habsburg*, Longman, 1963; Papermac, 1981.
5 Drage, G., *Austria–Hungary*, John Murray, 1909.
6 Eisenmann, L., 'Austria–Hungary, 1859–1909', in *The Cambridge Modern History*, vol. 11 Cambridge University Press, 1910.
7 Flesch-Brunningen, H., *Die letzten Habsburger in Augenzeugenberichten*, Deutscher Taschenbuch Verlag, 1982.
8 Gordon, H. and Gorden, N. (eds), *The Austrian Empire. Abortive Federation?* D.C. Heath, 1974.
9 Hantsch, H., *Die Geschichte Österreichs*, vol. 2, Styria Steirische Verlagsanstalt, 1947.
10 Jászi, O., *The Dissolution of the Habsburg Monarchy*, University of Chicago Press, 1929.
11 Kann, R.A., *The Multinational Empire. Nationalism and National Reform in the Habsburg Monarchy, 1848–1918*, 2 vols., Columbia University Press, 1950.
12 Kann, R.A., *History of the Habsburg Empire, 1526–1918*, University of California Press, 1974.
13 Kleinwaechter, F., *Der Untergang der österreichisch-ungarischen Monarchie*, Leipzig, 1920.
14 Kohn, H., *The Habsburg Empire, 1804–1918*, Van Nostrand, 1961.
15 Macartney, C.A., *The Habsburg Empire, 1790–1918*, Weidenfeld and Nicholson, 1969.
16 May, A.J., *The Hapsburg Monarchy, 1867–1914*, Harvard University Press, 1951.
17 Redlich, J., *Emperor Francis Joseph of Austria*, Macmillan, 1929.

18 Remak, J., 'The healthy invalid: how doomed was the Habsburg Empire?', *Journal of Modern History*, 41 (1969).

19 Steed, H.W., *The Habsburg Monarchy*, Constable, 1913.

20 Tapié, V.L., *The Rise and Fall of the Habsburg Monarchy*, Pall Mall Press, 1971.

21 Taylor, A.J.P., *The Habsburg Monarchy, 1809–1918,* Hamish Hamilton, 1948; Penguin, 1964.

22 Tihany, L.C., 'The Austro–Hungarian Compromise, 1867–1918: a half century of diagnosis; fifty years of post-mortem', *Central European History*, 2 (1969).

23 Wandruszka, A. and Urbanitsch, P. *Die Habsburgermonarchie, 1848–1918,* 3 vols., Österreichische Akademie der Wissenschaften, 1973–80.

24 Wangermann, E. *The Austrian Achievement, 1700–1800* Thames and Hudson, 1973.

MEMOIRS AND PERSONAL ACCOUNTS

25 Baernreither, J.M., *Fragments of a Political Diary*, ed. J. Redlich, Macmillan, 1930.

26 Bahr, H., *Selbstbildnis*, Fischer Verlag, 1923.

27 Braunthal, J., *In Search of the Millenium* Gollancz, 1945.

28 Clare, G., *Last Waltz in Vienna. The Destruction of a Family,1842–1942*, Macmillan, 1981.

29 Redlich, J., *Schicksalsjahre Österreichs, 1908–1919. Das Politische Tagebuch Josef Redlichs*, 2 vols., Bohlaus Verlag, 1953.

30 Steed, H.W., *Through Thirty Years*, 1892–1922, 2 vols., Heinemann, 1924.

31 West, R., *Black Lamb and Grey Falcon*, Macmillan, 1942.

32 Zweig, S., *The World of Yesterday*, Cassell, 1943.

ECONOMIC

33 Ashworth, W., 'Typologies and evidence: has nineteenth century Europe a guide to economic growth?' *Economic History Review*, xxx (1977).

34 Berend, I. and Ránki, G., 'Economic factors in nationalism: the example of Hungary at the beginning of the twentieth century', *Austrian History Yearbook*, 3 (1967).

35 Berend, I. and Ránki, G., *Hungary, A Century of Economic Development*, David and Charles, 1974.

36 Brusatti, A., 'Die Wirtschaftlichen Folgen des Ausgleichs von 1867', *Der Österreich-Ungarische Ausgleich von 1867: Vorgeschichte und Wirkungen*, ed. P. Berger, Herold, 1967.

37   Eddie, S.M., 'The changing pattern of landownership in Hungary, 1867–1914', *Economic History Review*, xx (1967).

38   Eddie, S.M., 'Agricultural production and output per worker in Hungary, 1870–1913', *Journal of Economic History*, xxviii (1968)

39   Eddie, S.M., 'The terms and patterns of Hungarian foreign trade, 1882–1913', *Journal of Economic History*, xxxvii (1977).

40   Gerschenkron, A., *Economic Backwardness in Historical Perspective*, Harvard University Press, 1962.

41   Gerschenkron, A., *An Economic Spurt That Failed*, Princeton University Press, 1977.

42   Good, D.F., 'Stagnation and Take-Off in Austria, 1873–1913', *Economic History Review*, xxvii (1974).

43   Good, D.F., 'Financial integration in late nineteenth century Austria', *Journal of Economic History*, xxxvii (1977).

44   Good, D.F., 'The Great Depression and Austrian growth after 1873', *Economic History Review*, xxxi (1978).

45   Good, D.F., 'Economic integration and regional development in Austria–Hungary, 1867–1913', in *Disparities in Economic Development*, ed. P. Bairoch and M. Levy-Leboyer, Macmillan, 1981.

46   Hertz, F., *The Economic Problem of the Danubian States*, Gollancz, 1949.

47   Gross, N.T., 'The Industrial Revolution in the Habsburg Monarchy, 1750–1914', in *The Fontana Economic History of Europe*, vol. 4, ed. C. Cipolla, Fontana, 1973.

48   März, E., 'Some economic aspects of the nationality conflict in the Habsburg Empire', *Journal of Central European Affairs*, xiii (1949).

49   Matis, H., *Österreichs Wirtschaft, 1848–1913*, Duncker and Humblot, 1972.

50   Mommsen, H., *Die Sozialdemokratie und die Nationalitäten im habsburgischen Vielvölkerstaat*, Europa Verlag, 1963.

51   Ránki, G., 'Problems of the development of Hungarian industry, 1900–1944', *Journal of Economic History*, xxiv (1964).

52   Rosenberg, H. 'Political and social consequences of the Great Depression, 1873–1896', *Economic History Review*, xiii (1943).

53   Rosenberg, H., *Grosse Depression und Bismarckzeit. Wirtschaftsablauf, Gesellschaft und Politik in Mitteleuropa*, De Gruyter, 1967.

54   Rudolph, R.L., 'Austria, 1800–1914', in *Banking and Economic Development*, ed. R. Cameron, Oxford University Press, 1972.

55   Rudolph., R.L., 'The pattern of Austrian industrial growth

from the Eighteenth to the Early Twentieth Century', *Austrian History Yearbook*, xi (1975).

56   Rudolph, R.L., *Banking and Industrialization in Austria–Hungary, The Role of Banks in the Industrialization of the Czech Crownlands, 1873–1914*, Cambridge University Press, 1976.

57   Sugar, P.R., *Industrialization of Bosnia–Hercegovina, 1878–1918*, University of Washington Press, 1963.

POLITICAL

(a) Nationalities

58   Beneš, V., 'The Slovaks in the Habsburg Empire: a struggle for existence', *Austrian History Yearbook*, 3, ii (1967).

59   Djordjević, D, 'The Serbs as an integrating and disintegrating factor', *Austrian History Yearbook*, 3, ii (1967).

60   Fischer-Galati, S., 'The Rumanians and the Habsburg Monarchy', *Austrian History Yearbook*, 3, ii (1967).

61   Greenfield, K.R., 'The Italian nationality problem of the Austrian Empire', *Austrian History Yearbook*, 3, ii (1967).

62   Hanák, P., 'Economics, society and sociopolitical thought in Hungary during the age of capitalism', *Austrian History Yearbook*, xi (1975).

63   Hanák, P., 'Hungary in the Austro–Hungarian Monarchy: preponderancy or dependency?', *Austrian History Yearbook*, 3, i (1967).

64   Havránek, J.,'The development of Czech nationalism', *Austrian History Yearbook*, 3, ii (1967).

65   Hoffman, G.W., 'The political-geographic bases of the Austrian nationality problem'. *Austrian History Yearbook*, 3, ii (1967).

66   Holotík, P., 'The Slovaks: an integrating or a disintegrating force?, *Austrian History Yearbook*, 3, ii (1967).

67   Janos, A., *The Politics of Backwardness in Hungary, 1825–1945*, Princeton University Press, 1982.

68   Jelavich, C., 'The Croatian problem in the Habsburg Empire in the nineteenth century', *Austrian History Yearbook*, 3, ii (1967).

69   Jenks, W.A., *Austria under the Iron Ring, 1879–1893*, University of Virginia Press, 1965.

70   Kann, R.A., 'The Austro–Hungarian Compromise of 1867 in retrospect. Cause and effect', in *Der Österreichisch-Ungarisch Ausgleich 1867*, ed. L. Holotík, Bratislava, 1971.

71 Kogan, A.G., 'The Social Democrats and the conflict of nationalities in the Habsburg Monarchy', *Journal of Modern History*, 21 (1949).

72 Konirsh, S., 'Constitutional aspects of the struggle between Germans and Czechs in the Austro–Hungarian Monarchy', *Journal of Modern History*, 27 (1955).

73 Krizman, B., 'The Croatians in the Habsburg Monarchy in the nineteenth century', *Austrian History Yearbook*, 3, ii (1967).

74 Macartney, C.A., *National States and National Minorities*, Royal Institute of International Affairs, 1934.

75 Macartney, C.A., *Hungary. A Short History*, Edinburgh University Press, 1962.

76 Rudnytsky, I., 'The Ukrainians in Galicia under Austrian rule', *Austrian History Yearbook*, 3, ii (1967).

77 Thomson, S.H., *Czechoslovakia in European History*, Princeton University Press, 1953.

78 Vucinich, W.S., 'The Serbs in Austria–Hungary', *Austrian History Yearbook*, 3, ii (1967).

79 Vyšný, P., *Neo–Slavism and the Czechs 1898–1914*, Cambridge University Press, 1977.

80 Wandycz, P.S., 'The Poles in the Habsburg Monarchy', *Austrian History Yearbook*, 3, ii (1967).

81 Whiteside, A., 'The Germans as an integrative force in Imperial Austria: the dilemma of dominance', *Austrian History Yearbook*, 3, i (1967).

82 Winters, S.B., 'The Young Czech Party, 1874–1914: an appraisal', *Slavic Review*, xxvii (1967)

83 Wiskemann, E., *Czechs and Germans*, Oxford University Press, 1938.

84 Zöllner, E., 'The Germans as an integrating and disintegrating Force', *Austrian History Yearbook*, 3, i (1967).

85 Zwitter, F., 'The Slovenes in the Habsburg Monarchy', *Austrian History Yearbook*, 3, ii (1967).

(b) Collapse of Liberalism

86 Bottomore, T. and Goode, P. (eds.), *Austro–Marxism*, Oxford University Press, 1978.

87 Boyer, J.W., 'Freud, marriage, and late Viennese liberalism: a commentary from 1905', *Journal of Modern History*, 50 (1978).

88 Boyer, J.W., *Political Radicalism in Late Imperial Vienna. Origins of the Christian Social Movement, 1848–1897*, University of Chicago, 1981.

89   Boyer, J.W., 'Karl Lueger and the Viennese Jews', *Leo Baeck Institute Yearbook*, xxvi (1981).

90   Cole, G.D.H., *A History of Socialist Thought*, vol. 3, pt.1: *The Second International, 1889–1914*, Macmillan, 1956.

91   Fraenkel, J. (ed.), *The Jews of Austria: Essays on Their Life, History and Destruction*, Valentine Mitchell, 1967.

92   Kornberg, J., 'Theodore Herzl: a reevaluation', *Journal of Modern History*, 52 (1980).

93   Leser, N., 'Austro-Marxism: a reappraisal', *Journal of Contemporary History*, 11 (1976).

94   Pulzer, P.G.J., 'The Austrian Liberals and the Jewish question, 1867–1914', *Journal of Central European Affairs*, 23 (1963).

95   Pulzer, P.G.J., *The Rise of Political Anti-Semitism in Germany and Austria, 1867–1938*, John Wiley, 1964.

96   Pulzer, P.G.J., 'The development of political anti-semitism in Austria', in *The Jews in Austria*, ed. J. Fraenkel. 1967.

97   Schorske, C., *Fin-de-Siècle Vienna*, University of Cambridge, 1981.

98   Stewart, D., *Theodor Herzl*, Hamish Hamilton, 1974.

99   Torrance, J., 'The emergence of sociology in Austria', *European Journal of Sociology*, xvii, 2 (1976).

100 Vital, D., *The Origins of Zionism*, Oxford University Press, 1975.

101 Whiteside, A.G., *The Socialism of Fools. Georg von Schönerer and Austrian Pan Germanism*, University of California Press, 1975.

CULTURE

102 Barea, I., *Vienna*, Secker and Warburg, 1966.

103 Bronsen, D., *Joseph Roth, Eine Biographie*,Deutscher Taschenbuch Verlag, 1981.

104 Crankshaw, E., *Vienna: the Image of a City in Decline*, Macmillan, 1938.

105 Field, F., *The Last Days of Mankind: Karl Kraus and His Vienna*, Macmillan, 1967.

106 Fuchs, A., *Geistige Strömungen in Österreich, 1867–1918*, Globus Verlag, 1949.

107 Heller, E., 'Karl Kraus: satirist in the modern world', in *The Disinherited Mind*, Bowes and Bowes, 1975.

108 Janik, A. and Toulmin, S., *Wittgenstein's Vienna*, Simon and Schuster, 1973.

109 Johnston, W.M., *The Austrian Mind. An Intellectual and Social History, 1848–1938*, University of California Press, 1972.

110   Johnston, W.M., *Vienna, Vienna, The Golden Age 1815–1914*, Clarkson N. Potter, 1981.

111   McGrath, W.J., *Dionysian Art and Populist Politics in Austria*, Yale University Press, 1974.

112   Magris, C., *Der habsburgische Mythos in der österreichischen Literatur*, Otto Müller Verlag, 1966.

113   Miller, J. (ed.), *Freud, the Man, his World, his Influence*, Weidenfeld and Nicolson, 1972.

114   Morton, F., *A Nervous Splendour. Vienna 1888/1889*, Penguin, 1980.

115   Powell, N., *The Sacred Spring, The Arts in Vienna, 1898–1918*, Studio Vista, 1974.

116   Redlich, H.F., *Bruckner and Mahler*, J.M. Dent, 1963.

117   Schnitzler, H., 'Gay Vienna – myth and reality', *Journal of the History of Ideas*, xv, 1 (1954).

118   Schorske, C., 'Generational tension and cultural change: reflections on the case of Vienna', *Daedalus*, 107 (1978).

119   Swales, M., *Arthur Schnitzler. A Critical Study*, Oxford University Press, 1971.

120   Szasz, T., *Karl Kraus and the Soul Doctors*, Routledge and Kegan Paul, 1977.

121   Vergo, P. *Art in Vienna, 1898–1918*, Phaidon, 1975.

122   Whitford, F., *Egon Schiele*, Thames and Hudson, 1981.

123   Williams, C.E., *The Broken Eagle. The Politics of Austrian Literature from Empire to Anschluss*, Elek, 1974.

Fiction

124   Kraus, K., *Die letzten Tage der Menschheit*, (1922) 2 vols., Deutscher Taschenbuch Verlag, 1964.

125   Musil, R., *Die Verwirrungen des Zöglings Törless*, (1960), English translation, *Young Torless*, Panther, 1971.

126   Roth, J., *Radetzkymarsch*, (1932), Deutscher Taschenbuch Verlag, 1981.

127   von Saar, F., *Dissonanzen*, (1900); Reclam, 1981.

128   von Saar, F., *Die Familie Worel*, (1904); Reclam, 1981.

129   Schnitzler, A., *Der Weg ins Freie*, (1908); Fischer Taschenbuch Verlag, 1978.

FOREIGN POLICY

130   Bridge, F.R., *From Sadowa to Sarajevo. The Foreign Policy of Austria–Hungary, 1866–1914*, Routledge and Kegan Paul, 1972.

Documents

131 Dedijer, V., 'Sarajevo fifty years after', *Foreign Affairs*, 42 (1964).

132 Dedijer, V., *The Road to Sarajevo*, MacGibbon and Kee, 1967.

133 Geiss, I. (ed.), *July 1914*, Batsford, 1967.

134 Grenville, J.A.S., 'Goluchowski, Salisbury, and the Mediterranean Agreements, 1895–97', *Slavonic and East European Review*, 36 (1958).

135 Jelavich, B., 'Foreign policy and the national question in the Habsburg Empire: a memorandum of Kálnoky', *Austrian History Yearbook*, 6 (1970).

136 Klein, F. (ed.), *Österreich–Ungarn in der Weltpolitik, 1900–1918*, Akademie Verlag, 1965.

137 Pribram, A.F., *The Secret Treaties of Austria–Hungary, 1879–1914*, 2 vols., Harvard University Press, 1920.

138 Pribram, A.F., *Austrian Foreign Policy, 1908–18*, Allen and Unwin, 1923.

139 Schmitt, B., *The Annexation of Bosnia, 1908–1909*, Cambridge University Press, 1937.

140 Schmitt, H.A., 'Count Beust and Germany, 1866–1870. Reconquest, realignment or resignation', *Central European History*, 1 (1968).

141 Seton-Watson, R.W., *The Southern Slav Question and the Habsburg Monarchy*, Constable, 1911.

142 Seton-Watson, R.W., 'The role of Bosnia in international politics, 1875–1914', *Proceedings of the British Academy*, xvii (1931).

143 Stone, N., 'Army and society in the Habsburg Monarchy, 1900–1914', *Past and Present*, 33 (1966).

144 Stone, N., 'Hungary and the crisis of July 1914', *Journal of Contemporary History*, 1 (1966).

145 Stone, N., 'Moltke–Conrad: relations between the Austro-Hungarian and German General Staffs, 1909–1914', *Historical Journal*, ix. (1966).

146 Wank, S., 'Aehrenthal's programme for the constitutional transformation of the Habsburg Monarchy: three secret Mémoires', *Slavonic and East European Review*, 41 (1963).

147 Wank, S., 'Aehrenthal and the Sanjak of Novibazar railway project: a re-appraisal', *Slavonic and East European Review*, 42 (1964).

148 Wank, S., 'Foreign policy and the nationality problem in Austria–Hungary, 1867–1914', *Austrian History Yearbook*, 3, iii (1967)

149   Williamson, S.R., 'Influence, power and the policy process: the case of Franz Ferdinand, 1906–1914', *Historical Journal*, 17 (1974).

WORLD WAR ONE AND THE COLLAPSE OF THE EMPIRE

150   Craig, G.A., 'The World War I alliance of the Central Powers in retrospect: the military cohesion of the alliance', *Journal of Modern History*, 37 (1965).

151   Fellner, F., 'The dissolution of the Habsburg Monarchy and its significance for the new order in Central Europe: a reappraisal', *Austrian History Yearbook*, 4–5 (1968).

152   Glaise-Horstenau, E., *The Collapse of the Austro–Hungarian Empire*, J.M. Dent, 1930.

153   Hanak, H., 'The New Europe, 1916–20', *Slavonic and East European Review*, 39 (1961)

154   Holborn, H., 'The final disintegration of the Habsburg Monarchy', *Austrian History Yearbook*, 3, iii (1967).

155   Kohn, H., 'Was the collapse inevitable?', *Austrian History Yearbook*, 3, iii (1967).

156   Namier, L.B., 'The downfall of the Habsburg Monarchy', in *Vanished Supremacies*, Penguin, 1962.

157   Rothenberg, G.E., 'The Habsburg army in the first World War, 1914–18', in *The Habsburg Empire in World War I*, ed. B. Kiraly, Columbia University Press, 1977.

158   Seton-Watson,H. and Seton-Watson, C., *The Making of a New Europe. R.W. Seton-Watson and the last years of Austria–Hungary*, Methuen, 1981.

159   Silberstein, G., 'The High Command and diplomacy in Austrian–Hungary, 1914–16', *Journal of Modern History*, 42 (1970).

160   Stadler, K.R., 'The disintegration of the Austrian Empire', *Journal of Contemporary History*, 3 (1968).

161   Stone, N., *The Eastern Front, 1914–1917*, Hodder and Stoughton, 1975.

162   Valiani, L., *The End of Austria–Hungary*, Secker and Warburg, 1973.

163   Zeman, Z.A.B., *The Break-Up of the Habsburg Empire, 1914–1918, A Study in National and Social Revolution*, Oxford University Press, 1961.

Index